W9-BLG-380

~ *The* ~
FARM HOME
Cookbook

Wholesome and Delicious
Recipes from the Land

Elsie Kline

Garden & Food Editor of *Farming Magazine*

Fountaindale Public Library
Bolingbrook, IL
(630) 759-2102

STREET
BOOKS

LANCASTER,
PENNSYLVANIA

The Farm Home Cookbook: Wholesome and Delicious Recipes from the Land

Copyright ©2018 by Elsie Kline

Softcover International Standard Book Number: 9781947597037

Library of Congress Control Number: Data available

Design by Cliff Snyder

Food photos by Dreamstime

Farm photos by *Farming Magazine*

The Farm Home Cookbook: Wholesome and Delicious Recipes from the Land is published by
Walnut Street Books, Lancaster, Pennsylvania
info@walnutstreetbooks.com

All rights reserved. Printed in the United States of America. No part of this book may be
reproduced in any form or by any means without the prior written permission of the publisher,
except for brief quotations in connection with reviews written specifically for inclusion in
magazines or newspapers or limited excerpts strictly for personal use.

Every effort has been made to assure that the recipes included in this book are accurate.
Neither Walnut Street Books, Elsie Kline, nor *Farming Magazine* will be responsible
for errors, whether typographical or otherwise.

Contents

A Meal-Time Song

This song was introduced to us years ago when our children were young and we sometimes sang it after meals. We sing it to the tune of "All Through the Night," which I often sang to the children when I was rocking them to sleep.

"For the Fruit of All Creation"

For the fruit of all creation
Thanks be to God.
For the gifts to every nation
Thanks be to God.
For the plowing, sowing, reaping
Silent growth while we are sleeping
Future needs in earth's safekeeping
Thanks be to God.

In the just reward of labor
God's will be done.
In the help we give our neighbor
God's will be done.
In our worldwide task of caring
For the hungry and despairing
In the harvest we are sharing
God's will be done.

For the harvests of the Spirit
Thanks be to God.
For the good we all inherit
Thanks be to God.
For the wonders that astound us
For the truths that still confound us
Most of all, that love has found us
Thanks be to God.

— *Words: Fred Pratt Green*

© 1970 Hope Publishing Company, Carol Stream, IL 60188. All rights reserved. Used by permission.

About This Cookbook

The recipes we've selected for this cookbook meet the criteria we use ourselves in cooking. I firmly believe that if we emphasize good, wholesome food and take pleasure in preparing it, a family meal can be an almost sacred ritual.

If we know where everything on the table comes from, we do not take our food for granted. It is meaningful to eat popcorn that we grew, drink grape juice from our own vines, and enjoy a good steak from our own home-raised steer, plus all the bounty from our gardens.

I speak for many when I say it is very gratifying to have our own bees for honey, make our own maple syrup or buy it from friends in the community, have our own milk, eggs, oatmeal, and most of our fruit.

I realize that not everyone can have their own gardens, and raise their own meat and eggs, but there are farmers who will gladly do it for you.

The recipes in this collection are our own family favorites, as well as many choice recipes that we've featured through the years in *Farming Magazine*. They call for no mixes, packaged whipped toppings, margarine, or processed foods. Not only

does fresh, wholesome food taste wonderful, it provides a good example for teaching our families to be thrifty, creative, and self-reliant.

In 1998, the threshing crew was eating dinner around the table in our farmhouse kitchen when the conversation first came up. "There just aren't any farm magazines that truly address small-scale farming," said one. Another chimed in, "Someone should start one." Then we moved to other topics, but the seed was sown.

A year later the subject was raised again, more seriously this time. Everyone had ideas about what they'd like to see in a magazine for farmers, including the two girls who were part of the crew.

My husband David and I, plus Leroy Kuhns as the driving force behind us, finally decided, "Why don't we go for it? Let's put our heads together and come up with a plan." Our foremost goal was to create a magazine that stresses sustainable living—and that radiates hope and optimism for the wide range of small-scale farming. We agreed that the publication should have a section especially for women—and why not food since it's an important subject for men as well. (They're always hungry, aren't they?) So the "Farm Home" pages in *Farming Magazine* were born.

We decided to feature a cookbook in each issue and share some recipes from that cookbook. The first issue of *Farming Magazine* was published in 2001, so by now we have quite a collection of recipes from the last 17 years.

Putting this cookbook together was quite a project, and I would never have accomplished it without help from many talented people. First of all, thank you to all who provided a cookbook to be featured in *Farming Magazine*. Thank you for all the recipes you shared with me, and my thanks, too, goes to everyone who tested these recipes. Thank you Merle Good, Phyllis Pellman Good, and Margaret High, whose expertise in publishing is the reason this project was even considered. And special thanks to my family for encouraging me to keep at it.

Being stewards of the soil and having the opportunity to live on a small-scale farm is a God-given blessing. Being surrounded by a loving community is something we cannot appreciate enough.

I write a small piece entitled "The Farm Home" in each issue of *Farming Magazine,* and scattered throughout the cookbook are excerpts from those pieces—thoughts about life, community, the farm, family, and God. I hope it gives you a view of life on our farm.

Joyful cooking,
Elsie Kline

The "Farm Home" Cookbook

BREAKFASTS *and* SUPPERS

Buttermilk Pancakes

2 eggs
2 cups buttermilk
1 tsp. baking soda
2¼ cups all-purpose flour
2 tsp. baking powder
1 tsp. salt
4 Tbsp. (half stick) melted butter
maple syrup, for serving

Makes:

15 pancakes

Prep. Time:

10 minutes

1. In a mixing bowl, beat eggs until light. Add buttermilk and baking soda.

2. Separately, whisk together flour, baking powder, and salt. Stir flour mixture into egg mixture.

3. Add melted butter. Beat until smooth.

4. Fry on a hot, lightly greased griddle. Flip pancakes when they puff up a bit and bubbles rise to the surface and break. Fry on second side until nicely browned.

Serve hot with maple syrup.

Baked Apple Pancake

4 Tbsp. (half stick) butter, *divided*
3 apples, peeled, cored, and cut into thin wedges
1 cup all-purpose flour
1 cup milk
6 eggs
1 tsp. vanilla
½ tsp. salt
¼ tsp. nutmeg
confectioners sugar, for dusting

1. Place a 10" cast-iron skillet inside the oven and preheat oven to 450° while preparing the ingredients.

2. In another skillet, melt 2 Tbsp. butter. Add apples and sauté until they just begin to soften.

3. Remove from heat and set aside.

4. In a mixing bowl, blend flour, milk, eggs, vanilla, and salt together thoroughly.

5. Remove the hot skillet from the oven and add the remaining 2 Tbsp. butter.

6. Arrange the apples in the bottom of the skillet. Pour the batter over the apples.

7. Return to oven and bake for 15 minutes, then reduce heat to 375° and bake 10 more minutes.

8. Remove from oven and cool for 5 minutes before serving. Dust with confectioners sugar if desired.

Makes:

6-8 servings

Prep. Time:

20 minutes

Baking Time:

25 minutes

Cooling Time:

5 minutes

Variation:

Serve with maple syrup. The pancake can be inverted onto a large platter to serve if desired.

Finnish Pancake

¼ cup (half stick) + 1 Tbsp. butter, *divided*
4 eggs, well beaten
⅔ cup all-purpose flour
½ tsp. salt
1 Tbsp. butter
¼ cup sugar
2 cups milk
maple syrup, for serving

Makes:
___

6–8 servings

Prep. Time:
___

10 minutes

Baking Time:
___

20 minutes

1. Place ¼ cup butter in 9" × 13" baking pan. Place pan in oven and heat to 400°.

2. Meanwhile, mix the rest of ingredients, including remaining 1 Tbsp. butter, in mixing bowl. Whisk well.

3. Tilt baking pan so melted butter covers the bottom. Then pour batter on top of melted butter.

4. Return to oven and bake at 400° for 20 minutes or until browned and bubbly. Cut in squares. Serve with maple syrup.

Pancakes, Farm-Style

2½ cups all-purpose flour
1 tsp. salt
⅓ cup sugar *or* honey
2 tsp. baking powder
2 eggs
½ cup cornmeal
½ cup (1 stick) butter, melted
1½ cups milk

Makes:
___

16–18 pancakes

Prep. Time:
___

10 minutes

Variation:
___

If desired, add 1 cup whole corn. We call those fritters.

1. Combine flour, salt, sugar, and baking powder in a bowl.

2. Add eggs, cornmeal, and melted butter. Add milk and mix well to make a thick, pourable batter. Add more milk, 1 Tbsp. at a time, if needed for the right consistency.

3. Fry on a hot, lightly greased griddle. Flip pancakes when they puff up a bit and bubbles rise to the surface and break. Fry on second side until nicely browned. Serve hot.

Hearty Oatmeal Pancakes

2 cups rolled oats
2 cups buttermilk *or* plain yogurt
2 eggs, lightly beaten
¼ cup (half stick) melted butter
½ cup whole wheat flour
1 tsp. baking powder
½ tsp. cinnamon
½ tsp. salt

Makes:

5–6 servings

Prep. Time:

15 minutes

Resting Time:

12 hours or overnight

Variation:

Stir in blueberries or apples.

1. Twelve hours (usually overnight) before you want to make pancakes, mix together rolled oats and buttermilk or yogurt in a large bowl. Cover and refrigerate.

2. After 12 hours or overnight, mix together eggs and melted butter. Stir into oats mixture.

3. In a small bowl, mix together remaining dry ingredients. Add to oats mixture and stir briefly. The batter will be thick.

4. Fry on a hot, greased griddle over medium heat. Flip pancakes when they puff up a bit and bubbles rise to the surface and break. Fry on second side until nicely browned. Serve hot.

Blackberry Skillet Custard

1 tsp. butter

4 eggs, beaten

⅔ cup all-purpose flour

⅓ cup + 2 Tbsp. sugar, *divided*

¼ tsp salt

1 tsp. vanilla

1½ cups milk

2 cups blackberries

maple syrup, for serving

Makes:

8 servings

Prep. Time:

10 minutes

Baking Time:

40 minutes

1. Place butter in 12-inch cast iron skillet and put in oven. Heat oven to 350°.

2. In a mixing bowl, beat the eggs; add flour, ⅓ cup sugar, salt, and vanilla. Add milk and beat well.

3. Tilt the skillet so melted butter covers the bottom. Then pour batter into hot, greased skillet. Scatter berries on top. Sprinkle with remaining 2 Tbsp. sugar.

4. Bake 40 minutes until puffed and a knife inserted in center comes out clean. Serve warm with maple syrup. Sausages go well with this, too.

We farm people usually have our main meal at noon, a practice from when farmers did the fieldwork with teams of horses. You need to unhitch the horses at noon to water, feed, and rest them. So it just made sense for the family to eat their main meal and have a short siesta while the horses rested. Our schedule was to eat at 11:30 and then go back to work at 1. Since most of the heavy work was done before supper at 5, the big meal was needed at noon. Then we had dishes like corn pone and custard for supper. Usually salads, sliced tomatoes, and other garden vegetables were also served.

When men began working away from home, dinner slipped into supper. Dinner at noon became lunch, and supper vanished. When we had children in school and classes resumed in early September, we had the main meal at supper. That way the whole family shared in the main meal.

Spinach Frittata

2 strips bacon

1 cup thinly sliced scallions

2 cups fresh, torn spinach, washed and dried

3 eggs

½ tsp. salt

¼ cup milk

2 Tbsp. water

¼ cup grated sharp cheese

Makes:
_____

2 servings

Prep. Time:
_____

15 minutes

Cooking Time:
_____

15-20 minutes

1. In a medium skillet, fry bacon until crisp, 5-10 minutes. Remove to a paper towel to drain.

2. Add scallions to drippings in skillet and fry about 2 minutes, till softened.

3. Add spinach and cook 2 minutes more, until just wilted.

4. Beat eggs with salt, milk, and water.

5. Pour evenly over the vegetables, making sure the liquid spreads over the whole skillet.

6. Sprinkle with cheese. Cover pan and cook over low heat undisturbed to set the eggs and melt the cheese, about 8 minutes.

7. Serve hot or at room temperature with the reserved bacon. We like to have fresh bread with it, too.

Maine Wild Blueberry French Toast

12 slices (½" thick) firm-textured bread
4 oz. cream cheese, softened to room temperature
2–3 Tbsp. wild blueberry jam
5 eggs
¾ cup whole milk
½ cup cream
¼ tsp. nutmeg
½ tsp. vanilla
4 Tbsp. brown sugar, *divided*
½ cup coarsely chopped pecans
1 tsp. + 2 Tbsp. butter, *divided*
¼ tsp. salt
1 cup blueberries
confectioners sugar
maple syrup, for serving

Makes:

12–15 servings

Prep. Time:

35 minutes

Chilling Time:

8 hours

Standing Time:

40 minutes

Baking Time:

60–70 minutes

Note:

We've discovered that domestic Ohio blueberries work just fine, too.

1. Toast bread in toaster, or on a baking sheet in a 250° oven for 15 minutes on each side. Set aside to cool.

2. In a small bowl, mix cream cheese and jam.

3. Spread cream cheese mixture on half the bread slices and place the other slices on top, creating 6 sandwiches. Cut each sandwich in half diagonally.

4. Place in a buttered 9" × 13" baking dish.

5. In a mixing bowl, whisk together eggs, milk, cream, nutmeg, vanilla, and 2 Tbsp. brown sugar. Pour mixture evenly over sandwiches.

6. Cover pan with plastic wrap, pressing it down on the sandwiches in the liquid to make contact and reduce air.

7. Refrigerate at least 8 hours or overnight.

8. Allow baking dish to stand at room temperature for 30 minutes.

9. While the oven preheats to 350°, spread pecans, 1 tsp. butter, and salt on baking tray. Toast in oven until fragrant, 5-10 minutes.

10. Sprinkle pecan mixture and blueberries over sandwiches in baking pan.

11. Melt the remaining 2 Tbsp. butter and 2 Tbsp. brown sugar together. Drizzle over pecans and blueberries.

12. Bake at 400° covered for 30 minutes, then uncovered for 20-30 minutes, until top is bubbling.

13. Allow to stand for 10 minutes to firm up.

14. Sprinkle with confectioners sugar and serve with maple syrup or, better yet, Maine wild blueberry syrup.

Tip:

You can reduce this recipe by one-half or one-fourth. If you make only a one-fourth portion, use 1 Tbsp. blueberry jam; for half the recipe, use 1 ½-2 Tbsp. jam to maintain a strong blueberry flavor.

Breakfast Delight

2 cups rolled oats
1 cup water
¼ tsp. salt
¼ cup raisins
2 cups diced fresh apples
¼ cup chopped walnuts *or* almonds
2 Tbsp. honey
2 Tbsp. maple syrup
¼ tsp. cinnamon
¼ tsp. nutmeg
½ tsp. vanilla
milk *or* light cream, for serving

Makes:

5–6 servings

Prep. Time:

10 minutes

Cooking Time:

5–7 minutes

1. Combine the oats, water, and salt in medium saucepan. Bring to a boil and cook for 1–3 minutes.

2. Remove from heat and stir in everything else except the milk or cream.

3. Warm again on stove until steaming. Cover and let stand for several minutes to blend the flavors.

4. Then enjoy with milk or cream.

Today our daughters and daughters-in-law are coming home to help me with outside work. Our neighbors are having a wedding on Thursday, and the wedding services will be in our barn, with the reception at their place.

Our girls are even bringing our noon meal along today. It will be a good day, I'm sure!

Raccoon Valley Porridge

1 heaping Tbsp. flaxseed *or* rolled oats
2 heaping Tbsp. Cream of Wheat
½ cup Wheatena
small handful raisins
small handful walnuts
2 dried apricots, chopped
pinch salt
2 cups water

Makes:

2 servings

Cooking Time:

8 minutes

1. Combine all ingredients in saucepan. Then bring to boil and stir until thick, about 3 minutes.

2. Let stand with lid on for 5 minutes.

3. Serve with maple syrup or honey and milk.

A recipe that invites improvisation...

Corn Pone

2 cups cornmeal
1 cup all-purpose flour
1 tsp. baking soda
1 tsp. salt
½ cup sugar *or* honey
1 egg, beaten
1½ cups sour milk*
    or buttermilk
½ cup (1 stick) butter, melted

* Make your own sour milk by putting 1–2 Tbsp. apple cider vinegar into a one-cup measure. Fill the cup with milk. Stir gently. Allow to stand 2–3 minutes.

Makes:
6 servings

Prep Time:
15 minutes

Baking Time:
30 minutes

1. Mix cornmeal, flour, baking soda, and salt together. Set aside.

2. In a separate bowl, mix together sugar or honey, egg, and milk. Add melted butter. Mix well.

3. Add dry ingredients and mix well.

4. Put into a greased 8" × 8" baking pan.

5. Bake at 375° for 30 minutes, or until toothpick inserted in center comes out clean.

6. Serve with fruit and milk.

When we eat this as the main dish with milk and fruit at supper, we call it corn pone. All we have with it is some cheese, and of course, coffee. Other times when we eat it like a bread, we call it cornbread!

Earthbound Farm's Famous Maple Almond Granola

4½ cups rolled oats
¾ cup raw unsalted sunflower seeds
1½ cups slivered *or* chopped raw almonds
2 Tbsp. ground cinnamon
1¼ cups pure maple syrup
⅓ cup (5⅓ Tbsp.) butter, melted
1 cup raisins

Makes:

10 cups

Prep. Time:

15 minutes

Baking Time:

40-45 minutes

1. In mixing bowl, mix all ingredients—except raisins—together well.

2. Spread granola on rimmed baking sheet. Bake at 325° until it begins to brown, about 25 minutes, then stir with a flat spatula.

3. Continue to bake until light golden brown, 15 or 20 minutes longer. Stir occasionally during baking time, and watch carefully so it doesn't burn.

4. After cooling, add raisins. Store in airtight container.

Apple Grunt

¼ cup (half stick) butter,
   room temperature
1 cup sour milk*
   or buttermilk
2 eggs
1 tsp. vanilla
1 cup sugar
1 tsp. baking soda
1 tsp. salt
2 tsp. baking powder
1¼ cups all-purpose flour
2 cups chopped apples

Crumb Topping:
¾ cup brown sugar
1 tsp. cinnamon
3 Tbsp. all-purpose flour
3 Tbsp. butter

** Make your own sour milk
by putting 1-2 Tbsp. apple
cider vinegar into a one-
cup measure. Fill the cup
with milk. Stir gently. Allow
to stand 2-3 minutes.*

Makes:

6 servings

Prep. Time:

10 minutes

Baking Time:

30 minutes

1. Mix all Grunt ingredients, adding apples last.

2. Put in greased 8" × 8" baking pan.

3. Combine ingredients for crumbs and scatter on top of apple mixture.

4. Bake at 350° for 30 minutes, or until tester inserted into center of Grunt comes out clean. Serve with milk for supper or ice cream for dessert.

This is a favorite supper dish of ours. We eat it with milk and sliced Swiss cheese as a side dish. A doubled recipe fills a 9" x 13" baking pan.

Breakfast Casserole

8 slices bread, buttered

1 lb. cheddar cheese, grated

½ cup fried, chopped bacon

chopped bell peppers, onions, mushrooms, sliced black
   olives, *optional*

8 eggs

3 cups milk

¾ tsp. salt

¾ tsp. pepper

1. Cut buttered bread into 1" cubes.

2. Place in greased 9" × 13" baking pan.

Makes:

12–15 servings

Prep. Time:

25 minutes

Resting Time:

overnight

Baking Time:

1 hour

3. Sprinkle cheese and bacon over bread.

4. Scatter peppers, onions, mushrooms, and olives over top, if desired.

5. Separately, beat eggs well. Add milk and seasonings.

6. Pour egg mixture over bread cubes, cheese, bacon, and vegetables.

7. Cover. Refrigerate overnight.

8. The next morning, bake covered at 350° for 1 hour.

Sausage Cheese Biscuit Bake

2 cups all-purpose flour
1 tsp. salt
1 Tbsp. sugar
½ cup (1 stick) butter, melted
3 tsp. baking powder
1¼ cups milk, *divided*
1 Tbsp. minced onion
2 eggs
¼ tsp. salt
1½ cups shredded Monterey Jack cheese
8 oz. sliced sausage, uncooked
1 tsp. dried oregano, *or* 1 Tbsp. fresh chopped oregano

Makes:

6-8 servings

Prep. Time:

20 minutes

Baking Time:

25 minutes

Standing Time:

5 minutes

1. Make dough by combining flour, salt, sugar, butter, and baking powder in a good-sized bowl. Stir in ¾ cup milk until dough leaves sides of bowl.

2. Turn onto floured surface. Knead lightly 10 times.

3. Press dough on bottom and up sides of greased 10" × 15" jellyroll pan.

4. Bake at 425° for 8-10 minutes, until browned.

5. In a mixing bowl, beat remaining ½ cup milk with onion, eggs, and salt. Stir in cheese.

6. Pour and spread over baked crust.

7. Arrange sausage on top. Sprinkle with oregano.

8. Return to 425° oven and bake until set, about 15 minutes.

9. Let stand for 5 minutes before serving.

Frypan Toastwiches

2 cups cooked meat, such as chicken chunks, ground beef,
   beef chunks, *or* bulk sausage
¼ cup grated cheese of your choice
¼ cup mayonnaise
½ cup chopped pickles
butter
10-12 slices bread

Makes:

5-6 sandwiches

Prep. Time:

15 minutes

Cooking Time:

15 minutes

Note:

I use my home-canned meat for convenience.

1. In a bowl, break or crumble up meat if needed.

2. Add cheese, mayo, and pickles. Mix.

3. Butter bread.

4. Spread sandwich filling on the unbuttered sides, top with another slice of bread also with buttered side out.

5. Fry in pan until golden brown on each side.

Breakfast Egg and Basil Sandwich

1 English muffin, split
1 slice cheese
1 egg, fried *or* scrambled
1 tsp. prepared mustard, *or* to taste
fried ham, sausage, *or* bacon, *optional*
1 slice of fresh tomato
6-8 fresh basil leaves
4-6 fresh baby spinach leaves

Makes:

1 serving

Prep. Time:

10 minutes

Baking Time:

10 minutes

1. Toast and butter muffin.

2. Place cheese on bottom half of muffin; add egg and optional ham, sausage or bacon.

3. Spread a little mustard on top half of muffin. Place on top to make sandwich.

4. Wrap in foil and bake at 350° for 5-10 minutes, until hot and melty.

5. Pull open the muffin (careful—it's hot!) and add tomato, basil, and spinach.

Variation:

Homemade buns or bread serve just as well here as an English muffin.

Open-Faced Tomato Sandwich

bread
butter
honey
tomato slices
ground pepper
Swiss cheese, sliced
garlic salt, lettuce, fresh basil, fresh parsley, *optional*

1. Toast desired number of bread slices.

2. Spread each slice with butter and honey.

3. Add a slice of tomato, sprinkle of pepper, and a slice of Swiss cheese. Simple but delicious! Add any of the optional toppings—your choice.

Makes:

Serves as many as you want

Prep. Time:

10 minutes

Variation:

Use mayo on the toast instead of honey. Although it sounds unusual, we like honey on these sandwiches, a delicious touch of sweet and sour.

The "FARM HOME" Cookbook

BREADS

Blueberry Lemon Bread

½ cup (1 stick) butter, room
  temperature
1½ cups sugar
2 tsp. baking powder
½ tsp. salt
2 eggs
2 cups all-purpose flour
½ cup milk
1½ cups blueberries, fresh *or*
  frozen (no need to thaw)

Glaze:
¼ cup lemon juice
⅓ cup sugar

Makes:

2 loaves

Prep Time:

20 minutes

Baking Time:

50-60 minutes

1. In a mixing bowl, beat together butter and sugar.

2. Add baking powder and salt. Beat well.

3. Add eggs one at a time and beat well.

4. Add flour and milk alternately, stirring after each addition.

5. Stir blueberries in gently.

6. Divide batter between 2 greased 8" × 4" loaf pans.

7. Bake at 350° for about 50-60 minutes, until toothpick inserted in middle comes out clean. Meanwhile, mix lemon juice and sugar to make glaze. Set aside.

8. Run a knife around the baked loaves and tip out onto cooling rack. Prick tops with fork. Brush with glaze.

Delicious served warm.

Pumpkin Bread

½ cup (1 stick) butter, softened
1¾ cups maple syrup
4 eggs
2 cups cooked, pureed pumpkin
3½ cups all-purpose flour
½ tsp. baking powder
2 tsp. baking soda
1 tsp. cinnamon
1 tsp. ground cloves
1½ tsp. salt
¾ cup raisins
¾ cup chopped nuts

Makes:

2 loaves

Prep time:

15 minutes

Baking time:

65–75 minutes

1. In a mixing bowl, cream butter and maple syrup together. Then stir in eggs and pumpkin.

2. Blend in dry ingredients. Then stir in raisins and nuts.

3. Divide batter between two greased 9" × 6" loaf pans.

4. Bake at 350° for 65–75 minutes, or until tester inserted in centers of breads comes out clean.

My mother-in-law had a stove that always baked faster than mine. Sometimes if I happened to be busy in the fields and had bread dough that needed to be baked while I was out there, she would do it for me. It was always browner than I would have preferred, but I wouldn't have considered saying anything because I appreciated her doing it for me. Her stove showed the same temperature as mine did, and it was a better stove than mine was. Our daughter now has that stove and simply uses lower temperatures. And loves it.

Dipped Apple Muffins

3 cups all-purpose flour
½ tsp. cinnamon
½ tsp. nutmeg
1 cup sugar
½ tsp. salt
4 tsp. baking powder
⅔ cup (10⅔ Tbsp., *or* 1 stick +
    2⅔ Tbsp.) butter
2 eggs, beaten
½ cup milk
1 cup peeled, grated apple

For dipping:
melted butter
½ cup sugar
1 tsp. cinnamon

Makes:

15 to 20 muffins

Prep. Time:

20 minutes

Baking Time:

20-25 minutes

1. Mix dry ingredients together in a bowl.

2. Cut butter into dry ingredients with a pastry cutter or two knives.

3. Add eggs, milk, and grated apple. Mix just enough to moisten.

4. Spoon into greased muffin tins, filling half full. Or use paper cupcake liners within the muffin tins instead.

5. Bake at 350° for 20-25 minutes. When tester inserted into center of muffins comes out clean, the muffins are done.

6. Set up dipping station. Place melted butter in bowl. Mix cinnamon and sugar in another bowl.

7. Remove muffins from pan while still hot. Dip tops one-by-one into melted butter, then into cinnamon sugar mixture. Or brush the muffin tops with melted butter and then dip them into the cinnamon sugar.

Blueberry Scones

2 cups all-purpose flour
¼ cup sugar
1 Tbsp. baking powder
½ tsp. baking soda
¼ tsp. salt
¼ cup (half stick) butter
1 cup buttermilk
1 egg
1 tsp. vanilla
1 Tbsp. orange *or* lemon zest
1-2 cups blueberries

Glaze, *optional*
1 cup confectioners sugar
1 tsp. lemon juice
1 tsp. milk

Makes:
_____

10 large scones

Prep. Time:
_____

20 minutes

Baking Time:
_____

20-22 minutes

1. Mix dry ingredients in medium bowl.

2. With pastry blender, cut butter into dry ingredients until fine crumbs form.

3. Separately, mix buttermilk, egg, and vanilla in a small bowl.

4. Add to dry ingredients, stirring briefly just until mixed.

5. Fold in zest and blueberries.

6. For each scone, fill a ½-cup measure heaping full and drop onto baking sheet, allowing an inch or two between them.

7. Bake at 400° for 20-22 minutes. When tester inserted into centers of scones comes out clean, they're done.

8. Mix all glaze ingredients together and drizzle scones with it, or dust with confectioners sugar while still warm.

Biscuit Mix

5 lbs. all-purpose flour (up to half whole wheat flour may be used)
¾ cup baking powder
2 tsp. cream of tartar
3 Tbsp. salt
2 lbs. lard
⅓ cup sugar, *optional*

1. In a large bowl, mix all ingredients well with a pastry blender.

2. Store in an airtight container.

To make biscuits:

3. Combine 2 cups biscuit mix with 1 cup milk in mixing bowl.

4. Drop by tablespoons onto ungreased baking sheet or stone.

5. Bake at 400° for 10-12 minutes, or until light golden brown.

To make breadsticks:

6. Melt ¼ cup butter on rimmed baking sheet.

7. Combine 2 cups biscuit mix with ¾ cup milk in mixing bowl.

8. Turn onto floured board. Roll dough over to coat and knead lightly 10 times.

9. Roll ½" thick. Cut into ¾" wide strips to desired length.

10. Place on baking sheet with melted butter, turning and brushing the sticks to coat them.

11. Sprinkle with caraway, sesame, or poppy seeds, or garlic salt, or both.

12. Bake at 400° for about 15 minutes, or until lightly browned.

Makes:

10 batches of biscuits

Prep. Time:

20 minutes

Note:

This mixture keeps well for 2 months or more. Use like commercial Bisquick in recipes that call for it.

Cheddar and Chives Biscuits

2½ cups sprouted grain flour *or* all-purpose flour
2½ tsp. baking powder
½ tsp. baking soda
½ tsp. salt
½ cup (1 stick) butter, softened
1¼ cups buttermilk
½ cup shredded cheddar cheese
2 Tbsp. chopped chives, fresh *or* dried
2 Tbsp. (¼ stick) butter, melted

Makes:

12-15 biscuits

Prep. Time:

15 minutes

Baking Time:

10-12 minutes

1. Combine flour, baking powder, baking soda, and salt in a mixing bowl.

2. Cut in ½ cup butter with a pastry cutter or two knives until crumbs form.

3. Stir in buttermilk, cheese, and chives until blended.

4. Drop by heaping tablespoons 1" apart onto ungreased baking sheet.

5. Brush biscuits with 2 Tbsp. melted butter.

6. Bake 10-12 minutes at 450°.

7. Serve warm, spread with butter and honey.

Whole Wheat Tortillas

3 cups whole wheat flour
1 tsp. salt
⅓ cup olive oil
1 cup warm water

Makes:
_____

12 tortillas

Prep. Time:
_____

25–30 minutes

Rising Time:
_____

30 minutes

1. Mix flour and salt in bowl.

2. Add oil and warm water. Stir, using a fork, and work mixture into a soft dough.

3. Let rest for 30 minutes in covered bowl.

4. Cut into 12 pieces.

5. Roll each piece out paper-thin on slightly oiled counter.

6. Cook in non-stick skillet on both sides, 1 minute per side.

7. If not serving immediately, refrigerate or freeze the tortillas.

Popovers

2-3 Tbsp. softened butter for greasing muffin tins
1 cup all-purpose flour
4 eggs, room temperature
1 cup milk, room temperature
½ tsp. salt

1. Preheat oven to 400°.

2. Grease 12 muffin cups liberally with soft butter.

3. Beat together flour, eggs, milk, and salt until smooth.

4. Set muffin tin in hot oven for one minute.

5. Then divide batter evenly between each muffin cup and immediately place in pre-heated oven.

6. Bake for 35 minutes, resisting the urge to peek at them, as this may cause them to fall. When done, they will be puffed and golden brown.

7. Serve at once with butter and jam.

Makes:

12 popovers

Prep. Time:

10 minutes

Baking Time:

35 minutes

Note:

It's good to have ingredients at room temperature for buoyancy.

Delicious Homemade Bread

5¾ cups white bread flour, *divided*
3 cups whole wheat flour
1 Tbsp. salt
3 Tbsp. yeast
3 cups warm water

¾ cup lard
⅔ cup honey
soft butter, for brushing loaves

Makes:

4 8" loaves

Prep Time:

30 minutes

1. In a large mixing bowl, combine ¾ cup white bread flour, all of whole wheat flour, salt, and yeast. Stir with a whisk.

2. Separately, combine and stir the warm water, lard, and honey.

3. Pour water mixture into flour mixture and stir well with whisk.

4. Now add the remaining 5 cups white bread flour gradually, adding cup by cup and stirring after each addition.

5. Let rise for 20 minutes.

6. Knead for 5-10 minutes.

7. Shape into a ball, grease dough and bowl, place dough in bowl, then cover bowl with kitchen towel and allow to rise for 1 hour.

8. Punch down. Cut into four equal pieces.

9. Shape each piece into a loaf and place in greased 8" × 4" bread pans. Prick top of each loaf 6 times with fork.

10. Cover pans with kitchen towel. Allow to rise until double, approximately 30-45 minutes, or longer, depending on the weather.

11. Bake at 375° for 25-30 minutes until golden brown.

12. Tip loaves out of pans onto cooling rack. Brush each loaf with butter while warm.

Rising Time:

approximately 2 hours

Baking Time:

25-30 minutes

Here's how I shape my loaves: I take the amount of dough for 1 loaf, slap and shape it into a rectangle approximately 12" x 8". Then I roll it up and have the seam underneath. With the side of my hand, I chop 2" from each end, tucking the ends underneath.

Pizza Crust

1 cup warm (110°) milk
1 Tbsp. instant yeast
1 tsp. honey
1 tsp. salt
2 Tbsp. olive oil
2¼ cups whole wheat flour, *divided*, plus extra for dusting
pizza toppings, whatever you like

1. In a mixing bowl, dissolve yeast in warm milk.

2. Add honey, salt, and oil.

3. Stir in 2 cups flour until smooth.

4. Sprinkle dough with ¼ cup flour and knead a little in your hands.

5. Put on a 12" greased pizza pan, or on a 12" or 13" ungreased baking stone. Spread to rim with hands, dusting with flour to prevent stickiness.

6. Let rise 30 minutes.

7. Bake at 350° for 12 minutes. (I do not preheat my baking stone.)

8. Add toppings and bake again until cheese is melted and toppings are hot, approximately 8 minutes.

Makes:

4 servings

Prep. Time:

15 minutes

Rising Time:

30 minutes

Baking Time:

20 minutes

Note:

This makes a soft crust.

Variation:

Toppings can be added before baking, but the whole pizza must then be baked longer, until crust is golden around edges.

Bread Sticks

1½ cups warm (110°) water
1 Tbsp. yeast
1 Tbsp. + ½ cup (1 stick) butter, melted, *divided*
1 Tbsp. sugar
1 tsp. salt
4 cups all-purpose flour
3 Tbsp. olive oil
3 Tbsp. finely grated Parmesan cheese, plus more for sprinkling
1 tsp. garlic powder
1 Tbsp. dried parsley flakes
2 Tbsp. Italian seasoning
pizza sauce, for serving

Makes:

Serves 8

Prep. Time:

25 minutes

Rising Time:

50 minutes

Baking Time:

15-18 minutes

1. In a mixing bowl, dissolve yeast in warm water. Add 1 Tbsp. butter, sugar, and salt.

2. Stir in flour and knead for several minutes.

3. Place dough in bowl. Cover the bowl. Let rise until doubled, about 30 minutes.

4. Roll out to a 15" square on floured counter.

5. Cut dough into 1"-wide strips. Cut each strip into 3 pieces.

6. In a shallow bowl, combine ½ cup butter, olive oil, Parmesan cheese, and seasonings.

7. Dip each dough stick into butter mixture and place on greased baking sheet. Let rise 20-30 minutes.

8. Sprinkle with a bit more Parmesan cheese.

9. Bake at 350° for 15-18 minutes or until golden brown.

10. Serve with hot pizza sauce for dipping.

Cinnamon Rolls

2 Tbsp. yeast
½ Tbsp. + ½ cup sugar, *divided*
2½ cups warm (110°) water, *divided*
2 eggs, beaten
1 Tbsp. salt
¾ cup (1½ sticks) butter, melted, *divided*
5½-6 cups all-purpose flour
¼ cup brown sugar, *divided*
2 tsp. cinnamon, *divided*
1 batch Easy Penuche Frosting (see recipe on page 206)
½ tsp. maple flavoring

Makes:

3 dozen rolls

Prep. Time:

35 minutes

Rising Time:

approximately
2 hours

Baking Time:

25-30 minutes

1. In a mixing bowl, dissolve yeast and ½ T. sugar in ½ cup warm water for 5 minutes.

2. Add eggs, salt, ½ cup butter, remaining 2 cups warm water, remaining ½ cup sugar, and flour. Stir well after each addition.

3. Place dough in greased bowl. Cover and let rise until double.

4. Punch down, reform the dough ball, and let rise again.

5. Divide dough in half. On a greased countertop, pat out half the dough into a rectangle ¼" thick with greased hands, or roll it out with a rolling pin.

6. Spread with 2 Tbsp. melted butter, then sprinkle with 2 Tbsp. brown sugar and 1 tsp. cinnamon.

7. Roll up jelly-roll style, starting with a long edge. Slice roll into 1-inch-thick slices. Lay cut-side-down on greased baking sheets. Repeat with other half of dough.

8. Let rise a bit, about 30 minutes, then bake at 350° for 25 to 30 minutes.

9. Frost with Easy Penuche Frosting with ½ tsp. maple flavoring added.

Homemade Bagels

1 tsp. yeast
1¼ cups warm milk
¼ cup (half stick) butter, softened
2 Tbsp. honey
1 tsp. salt
1 egg yolk
3½–4¼ cups all-purpose flour, *or* 3–3½ cups whole wheat flour

1. In a mixing bowl, dissolve yeast in warm (110°) milk.

2. Add the butter, honey, salt, and egg yolk.

3. Mix well.

4. Stir in enough flour to form a soft dough.

5. Knead until smooth and elastic.

6. Place dough in a greased bowl. Cover and let rise about 1 hour until doubled.

7. Shape dough into balls—8 balls if using white flour and 6 balls if using wheat.

8. Push thumb through centers of each ball to form a 1" hole.

9. Place bagels on floured surface, cover, and let rest for 15 minutes.

10. In a large saucepan bring 2-3 quarts water to a boil.

11. Drop 3 or 4 bagels at a time into boiling water. Boil 1-2 minutes, turning once.

12. Remove with a slotted spoon and place on greased baking sheet.

13. Bake at 400° for 20-25 minutes.

Makes:

6-8 bagels

Prep. Time:

20-25 minutes

Rising Time:

1 hour, 15 minutes

Cooking & Baking:

25 minutes

Variation:

Raisins or blueberries can be added, as well as cinnamon or any desired spices or seasonings. Be creative!

Icebox Butterhorns

1 Tbsp. yeast

2 Tbsp. warm water

2 cups warm milk

½ cup sugar *or* honey

1 egg, beaten

1 tsp. salt

6 cups all-purpose flour, *divided*

¾ cup (1½ sticks) butter, melted, plus more for brushing

Makes:

24 butterhorns

Prep. Time:

30 minutes

Baking Time:

15-20 minutes

1. In a mixing bowl, dissolve yeast in warm (110°) water.

2. Add milk (110°), sugar, egg, salt, and 3 cups flour.

3. Beat until smooth.

4. Beat in ¾ cup butter and remaining flour.

5. Do not knead. Dough will be sticky.

6. Place in a greased bowl, cover, and refrigerate overnight.

7. The next day, punch dough down and divide in two.

8. On floured surface, roll into two 12" circles.

9. Cut each circle into 12 pie-shaped wedges.

10. Roll each wedge up, starting with the wide end first. Place each butterhorn point down on greased baking sheet.

11. Cover with kitchen towel. Let rise until double, about one hour.

12. Bake at 350° for 15-20 minutes, until golden.

13. Brush with butter while still warm.

My girls prefer the name "icebox" for these rolls. They think it sounds more wholesome and delicious than "refrigerator." These are the greatest!

Honey and Chive Butter

1 cup (2 sticks) unsalted butter, softened
2-3 Tbsp. snipped fresh chives
2-3 Tbsp. honey

1. Place all ingredients in a bowl.

2. Blend well.

3. Serve with warm, crusty bread.

Makes:

1 cup

Prep. Time:

10 minutes

Lavender Honey Butter

1 Tbsp. ground, dried lavender flowers
1 Tbsp. honey
½ cup (1 stick) butter, softened

1. Blend well in a bowl.

2. Spread on warm biscuits or scones.

Makes:

½ cup

Prep. Time:

10 minutes

The "Farm Home" Cookbook

SALADS *and* DRESSINGS

Spinach Salad with Strawberries, Nuts, and Cheese

½ lb. fresh baby spinach, rinsed and dried
1–1½ cups sliced strawberries
½ cup pecan *or* walnut halves, lightly toasted
4 oz. crumbled blue *or* feta cheese
2 Tbsp. balsamic *or* fruit vinegar
½ Tbsp. minced shallot
1 Tbsp. honey
1 tsp. fresh thyme leaves
⅛ tsp. dry mustard
¼ cup olive oil
salt and pepper to taste

Makes:
4–6 servings

Prep. Time:
15 minutes

1. Toss spinach with sliced strawberries, nuts, and cheese in large salad bowl.

2. Combine vinegar, shallot, honey, thyme, and mustard in blender. Blend for 30 seconds.

3. Add the oil, salt, and pepper and blend for another 30 seconds.

4. Drizzle over the salad and toss until the leaves are coated. Serve immediately.

Layered Garden Salad

1 head lettuce or equivalent leaf lettuce, chopped

1 small onion, chopped

2 cups shredded carrots

2 cups frozen peas, thawed

4 hard-cooked eggs, chopped

8 slices bacon, fried and chopped

1½ cups salad dressing (see recipe on page 64)

2 Tbsp. sugar or honey

cream or milk

½ cup grated cheese

Makes:

10 servings

Prep. Time:

20 minutes

Chilling Time:

8-12 hours

1. Layer lettuce, onion, carrots, peas, eggs, and bacon in a 9" × 13" dish in order given.

2. Separately, mix salad dressing and sugar. Add enough milk or cream to make a smooth consistency.

3. Spread over salad like a frosting.

4. Top with grated cheese. Refrigerate 8 to 12 hours before serving.

It's been a cool spring with an abundance of rain. But last summer was so dry, I can't complain about too much rain. It's been said, "All civilization depends on the top six inches of soil and the fact that it rains." Being caretakers of the soil is a privilege.

Summer Salad

1 medium cucumber, sliced thin
2 medium yellow summer squash, sliced thin
2 medium tomatoes, sliced, preferably paste tomatoes with less juice
1 small sweet onion, sliced

¼ cup oil
2 Tbsp. apple cider vinegar
2 Tbsp. lemon juice
1 tsp. dried basil
1 tsp. sugar
¼ tsp. salt
garlic salt

Makes:

6–8 servings

Prep. Time:

15 minutes

Comment:

A very colorful salad and delicious!

1. Arrange cucumber, squash, tomato, and onion slices on a serving platter.

2. Whisk rest of ingredients together in small bowl to make dressing.

3. Pour dressing over top and sprinkle with garlic salt.

4. Refrigerate until ready to serve.

Marinated Tomatoes

3 large tomatoes, sliced (using red and yellow tomatoes adds a nice touch)
¼ cup green onions, sliced
¼ cup snipped fresh parsley
1 clove garlic, minced
2 Tbsp. snipped fresh thyme
⅔ cup olive oil
¼ cup vinegar
2 tsp. Worcestershire sauce
3 Tbsp. brown sugar
1 tsp. salt
¼ tsp. black pepper

Makes:

10–12 servings

Prep. Time:

15 minutes

Marinating Time:

several hours or overnight

1. Place tomato slices in shallow serving container.

2. Top with onions, parsley, garlic, and thyme.

3. Make dressing by combining olive oil, vinegar, Worcestershire sauce, brown sugar, salt, and pepper.

4. Pour over tomatoes, herbs, and onion.

5. Cover. Refrigerate several hours or overnight.

Variation:

Simply sprinkle tomato slices with parsley, basil, sugar, pepper, and salt. Dribble olive oil and vinegar over all. Serve immediately.

Coleslaw

1 large head cabbage, shredded
1 small onion, chopped
1 cup diced celery
1 green or red bell pepper,
   diced

½ cup honey
½ cup apple cider vinegar
2 tsp. salt
1 tsp. celery seed

Makes:

15–18 servings

Prep. Time:

20 minutes

Chilling Time:

12 hours

1. Mix all ingredients.

2. Refrigerate for 12 hours before serving. Keeps several weeks.

We raise cabbage and store it in a root cellar over winter. Instead of buying lettuce in the winter, we have our own cabbage for coleslaw.

Big Bow Tie Salad

1 cucumber, sliced
1 zucchini, sliced
1 yellow summer squash, sliced
1 red bell pepper, sliced
1 green bell pepper, sliced
1 small red onion, minced
4 cups fresh broccoli florets
3 cups fresh cauliflower florets
2 pkgs. Italian dressing mix (see recipe on page 71)
4½ cups bow tie pasta, uncooked
¼ cup olive oil
¼ cup red wine vinegar
¾ tsp. salt
½ tsp. pepper

Makes:

20–24 servings

Prep. Time:

40 minutes

Refrigeration Time:

5 hours or overnight

1. Allow water to remain on vegetables from washing them. Place vegetables in large salad bowl.

2. Sprinkle with dressing mix. Toss.

3. Cover and refrigerate 5 hours or overnight.

4. After vegetables have marinated, cook bow tie pasta according to package directions.

5. Drain and rinse with cold water.

6. Add cooled pasta to marinated vegetables.

7. In a small bowl, whisk olive oil, vinegar, salt, and pepper together.

8. Pour over salad. Toss to coat.

Petit Pois Salad

3½ cups very young new peas
1 cup sour cream
2 scallions, finely chopped
6 slices bacon, fried crisp, crumbled
½ tsp. salt
freshly ground pepper, to taste

1. Cook peas until tender, about 5 minutes. Drain. Rinse with cold water. Drain.

2. Chill peas 1–2 hours.

3. Gently mix chilled peas with rest of ingredients. Serve.

Makes:

5–6 servings

Prep. Time:

10 minutes

Chilling Time:

1–2 hours

Potato Salad

about 10 large potatoes, to yield 12 cups shredded or diced
    cooked potatoes
2 Tbsp. finely chopped onion
1 doz. eggs, hard-boiled and shredded
1½ cups diced celery
3 cups salad dressing (see recipe page 64, or use Miracle Whip)
2 Tbsp. apple cider vinegar
3 tsp. salt
2 cups sugar
4 Tbsp. prepared mustard
1 tsp. celery seed

1. Cook potatoes in their skins until soft.

2. Refrigerate until cold. Peel, then shred or dice into a very large bowl. You should have 12 cups shredded or diced potatoes.

Makes:

20–25 servings

Prep. Time:

20 minutes

Cooking Time:

45 minutes

Cooling Time:

1 hour

More chilling
(if time allows):

12–24 hours

3. Gently stir in the onion, shredded eggs, and celery.

4. To make dressing, mix salad dressing, vinegar, salt, sugar, mustard, and celery seed. Mix well.

5. Stir dressing gently into potato mixture.

Flavor is best if mixed and refrigerated a day or so ahead of serving.

Making Hard-Boiled Eggs

I recently learned that if you crack eggs just a tiny bit before you cook them they're easier to peel. It really does work!

Put one layer of room-temperature eggs in a kettle, and cover with cold water. Turn on heat and bring to boil, uncovered. When boiling, put lid on kettle and turn to low. Boil for 14 minutes. Turn off heat; let set for 3 minutes. Put eggs under cold water and peel.

Corn and Black Bean Salad

2 cups cooked black beans, rinsed and drained

1 cup cooked corn kernels, fresh or frozen

1 cup diced tomato, about 1 large tomato

1 small red onion, diced

2 Tbsp. chopped fresh parsley

2 tsp. minced garlic

2 Tbsp. white vinegar

¼ cup extra-virgin olive oil

1 tsp. chili powder

¼ tsp. ground cumin

1 tsp. sugar

½ tsp. salt

¼ tsp. pepper

Makes:

6-8 servings

Prep. Time:

15-20 minutes

Chilling (if time allows):

1 hour

It is good to refrigerate for at least an hour before serving to blend the flavors.

1. Place the black beans, corn, tomato, onion, and parsley in a large bowl. Stir gently to combine.

2. Place the rest of the ingredients in a small bowl and whisk to combine.

3. Pour the dressing over the bean mixture and toss to coat.

Betty's Marinated Carrots

15-16 medium carrots
1 green bell pepper, chopped
1 small onion, sliced
2 Tbsp. olive oil

¼ cup tarragon vinegar
1 tsp. dried oregano
½ tsp. salt
¼ tsp. pepper

Makes:

10-12 servings

Prep. Time:

15 minutes

Cooking Time:

5-7 minutes

Marinating Time:

6-12 hours

1. Cut carrots into thick coins. Boil until just tender. Rinse with cold water to stop cooking.

2. Drain well. Place in bowl with other ingredients, mixing well.

3. Let stand in marinade 6 to 12 hours before serving. Serve cold.

My early garden is only 30 feet from the kitchen door. I find great satisfaction in going out with a bowl and gathering the makings for a fine meal that's eaten less than an hour later. It can't get much fresher than that.

Grape Salad

4 lbs. red grapes
8 oz. cream cheese, room
   temperature

½ cup sugar
½ cup honey
16 oz. sour cream

Makes:

10 servings

Prep. Time:

10 minutes

Chilling Time:

2 hours

1. Wash grapes and place in serving bowl.

2. Mix cream cheese, sugar, honey, and sour cream.

3. Pour over grapes and mix. Refrigerate—most refreshing when chilled.

We eat Grape Salad as a dessert, but it can also be a side dish for a luncheon or cookout. I often replace the sugar with more honey.

Scallion and Bean Salad

1 pound dry white beans
2 quarts water
4 scallions, sliced
2 cloves garlic, crushed
¼ cup fresh lemon juice
½ cup olive oil
salt and freshly ground pepper
4 cups loosely packed, chopped raw greens, such as kale, spinach,
   or escarole
fresh snipped parsley

Makes:

6-8 servings

Soaking Time:

overnight

Cooking Time:

1 hour

Prep. Time:

15 minutes

1. Soak beans in water overnight.

2. The next morning, drain beans. Add 2 quarts fresh water to cover.

3. Cook until tender, approximately 1 hour. Drain and cool.

4. Make dressing by combining scallions, garlic, lemon juice, olive oil, salt, and pepper.

5. Place greens and beans in large salad bowl. Pour dressing over. Stir.

6. Sprinkle with parsley.

7. Refrigerate several hours before serving.

Chilling (if time allows):

2-4 hours

Fruit Salad with Honey-Orange Dressing

1 cup plain yogurt
¼ cup mayonnaise
¼ cup honey
1 tsp. grated orange peel
¼ tsp. dry mustard
3 Tbsp. orange juice
1½ tsp. apple cider vinegar
4 cups assorted fruit — we use whatever's in season

Makes:

4-6 servings

Prep. Time:

15 minutes

1. Whisk together yogurt, mayonnaise, honey, orange peel, and dry mustard in small bowl until blended.

2. Gradually mix in orange juice and vinegar.

3. Toss fruit gently with dressing.

California Waldorf Salad

⅓ cup plain yogurt *or* sour cream
⅓ cup mayonnaise
1 tsp. grated lime zest
2 Tbsp. fresh lime juice
2 tsp. curry powder
1 Tbsp. honey *or* sugar
1 unpeeled apple, diced

½ cup thinly sliced celery
½ cup raisins
¾ cup seedless grapes, cut in half
½ cup pecans or walnuts
5 ounces (about 6 cups) baby spinach

Makes:

6–8 servings

Prep. Time:

15 minutes

1. Make dressing. In a small bowl, mix yogurt, mayo, lime zest, lime juice, curry powder, and honey. Whisk.

2. Place the apple, celery, raisins, grapes, and nuts in a large bowl.

3. Add about half the dressing and stir to combine.

4. Just before serving add the spinach and toss to combine. More dressing can be added if the salad is too dry.

Lettuce Salad with Chicken

¼ cup mayonnaise

¼ cup sour cream

2 Tbsp. cream

2 Tbsp. honey

1½ Tbsp. red wine vinegar

2 cups shredded lettuce

1 cup chopped broccoli

¼ cup sliced radishes

2 Tbsp. chopped celery

¼ cup chopped onion

¼ cup shredded carrots

½ cup shredded cheddar cheese

1 cup chopped boneless skinless chicken, pan-fried until tender

Makes:
_____

6–8 servings

Prep. Time:
_____

20 minutes

1. Make dressing by mixing mayo, sour cream, cream, honey, and vinegar together well.

2. Put rest of ingredients in salad bowl. Toss with dressing. Serve immediately.

I had a nicely established lettuce bed that was picture-perfect, and then our old coon hound decided to dig and roll in it. She knows better.

Doesn't it make you sick when your dedicated work is undone in five minutes? I can understand a storm, but a dog?!

Crunchy Chicken Salad

½ cup apple cider vinegar
½ cup olive oil
½ cup honey
1 head lettuce, cut up
1 cup grated cheddar cheese

1 cup chow mein noodles
½ cup raisins
2 cups cooked, diced chicken
¼ cup sliced almonds

Makes:
6 servings

Prep. Time:
20 minutes

Cooling Time:
20 minutes

1. In a small saucepan, bring vinegar, olive oil, and honey to a boil. Simmer 2 minutes.

2. Set aside to cool.

3. When cool, combine lettuce, cheese, noodles, raisins, chicken, and almonds in salad bowl.

4. Pour dressing over. Stir. Serve immediately.

Southwest Chicken Salad

4 6" flour tortillas
butter
1 lb. boneless chicken breast, cooked and cut in 1" cubes
½ cup shredded cheddar cheese
2 cups canned, *or* fresh cooked whole-kernel, corn
2 cups cooked black beans, drained and rinsed
2 cups chopped tomatoes
1 medium green bell pepper, diced
⅓ cup chopped green onions
8 cups salad greens
⅔ cup ranch dressing
4 tsp. barbecue sauce

1. Spread tortillas lightly with butter on each side.

2. Cut into ½-inch strips. Place on baking sheet.

3. Bake at 350° degrees for 25 minutes or until crispy. Set aside to cool.

4. In a salad bowl, mix chicken, cheese, corn, beans, tomatoes, peppers, onions, and greens.

5. Make dressing. Whisk together ranch dressing and barbecue sauce.

6. Just before serving, mix dressing with salad. Sprinkle with tortilla strips.

Makes:

10 servings

Prep. Time:

30 minutes

Baking Time:

25 minutes

Variation:

Some like sweet and sour dressing (see recipe page 72) just as well on this salad.

Bacon Chicken Salad

½ cup mayonnaise

5 Tbsp. barbecue sauce (see recipe on page 129)

3 Tbsp. minced onion

¼ tsp. Liquid Smoke

½ tsp. salt

¼ tsp. pepper

1½ lbs. boneless chicken breasts

10 bacon strips, cooked and crumbled

4 cups chopped fresh spinach

4 cups chopped lettuce

2 tomatoes, diced

shredded cheese, *optional*

Makes:

6 servings

Prep. Time:

25 minutes

Cooking Time:

30 minutes

1. Make dressing by mixing mayo, barbecue sauce, onion, Liquid Smoke, salt, and pepper together. Refrigerate until ready to serve.

2. Bake, grill, or fry chicken, whichever you prefer, or use leftover cooked chicken. Cube. Cool.

3. Fry bacon. Crumble.

4. Assemble salad. Mix spinach, lettuce, tomatoes, cheese if you wish, bacon, and chicken. Pour dressing over. Mix and enjoy.

Taco Salad

1 lb. ground beef
1 onion, chopped
1 pkg. taco seasoning (see recipe on page 271)
1 head lettuce, cut up
1-2 tomatoes, diced
2 cups grated Colby cheese
15-oz. can kidney beans, drained
12-oz. bag Doritos *or* corn chips, crushed
1 cup French dressing (see recipe on page 70)

1. In a skillet, brown beef and onion.

2. Stir in taco seasoning. Allow to cool at least 30 minutes.

3. In a salad bowl, mix lettuce, tomatoes, cheese, and beans. Stir in cooled beef mixture.

4. Stir in French dressing, or your choice of dressing, and chips just before serving.

Makes:

12-15 servings

Prep. Time:

15 minutes

Cooling Time:

30 minutes

Variations:

Use cheddar cheese instead of Colby. Use black beans instead of kidney beans. Add sliced radishes.

Homemade Salad Dressing (aka Miracle Whip)

1¾ cups water
½ cup apple cider vinegar
⅔ cup all-purpose flour
2 Tbsp. maple syrup
2 tsp. salt
1 egg
1 tsp. lemon juice
¾ cup (1½ sticks) butter, softened
1 tsp. prepared mustard

Makes:

about 3 cups

Prep. Time:

15 minutes

Cooking Time:

10 minutes

1. In medium saucepan, cook water, vinegar, and flour together until thick. Stir frequently.

2. Process the rest of the ingredients in blender on high until creamy.

3. Add cooked mixture and blend on high until creamy and thick.

This is the best homemade salad dressing (aka, Miracle Whip, a cooked version of mayonnaise with water and some extra vinegar and sweetener) I've ever made. It caters to those of us who prefer to use butter instead of vegetable oils. I use a rotary egg beater instead of a blender, and it works just fine.

Homemade Mayonnaise

1 egg, at room temperature
1 egg yolk, at room temperature
1 tsp. Dijon-type mustard
1½ Tbsp. lemon juice
2 Tbsp. honey, *optional*
generous pinch of sea salt
1 cup olive oil *or* sunflower oil

Makes:

a generous cup

Prep. Time:

10 minutes

1. In a deep mixing bowl, combine everything but the oil.

2. Whisk and while whisking, slowly drizzle in oil. Whisk briskly. Mixture should emulsify into mayonnaise.

More lemon juice, honey, and salt may be added to suit your taste.

Creamy Basil Dressing

1 cup mayonnaise
½ cup sour cream
3 Tbsp. tarragon vinegar
1 tsp. Worcestershire sauce
½ cup lightly packed fresh basil leaves
1 clove garlic
3-4 green onions, chopped
2 Tbsp. chopped chives
½ tsp. dry mustard
black pepper to taste

Makes:

about 2 cups

Prep. Time:

10 minutes

Combine all ingredients in a blender and process until smooth.

Creamy Cress Salad Dressing

⅔ cup olive oil

2 cups tightly packed watercress, chopped

6 scallions, finely chopped

½ tsp. salt, *or* to taste

1 tsp. freshly ground pepper

4 Tbsp. sour cream

1. Combine oil, watercress, scallions, salt, and pepper in a blender or bowl.

2. Using whisk, slowly add sour cream, blending thoroughly.

3. Refrigerate in airtight jar.

Makes:

2½ cups

Prep. Time:

10 minutes

Variation:

May use part plain yogurt instead of sour cream.

Celery Seed Dressing

½ cup olive oil

½ cup apple cider vinegar

3 Tbsp. salad dressing (or use recipe on page 64)

½ cup honey

2 tsp. prepared mustard

1 medium onion, finely chopped

1 tsp. salt

½ tsp. pepper

1 tsp. celery seed

Mix well, cover tightly, and store in refrigerator.

Makes:

1½ cups

Prep. Time:

10 minutes

Coleslaw Dressing

½ cup sugar
1½ Tbsp. all-purpose flour
1½ tsp. dry mustard
1 tsp. salt

1 egg
⅓ cup apple cider vinegar
½ cup water
1 cup sour cream

Makes:

about 2 cups

Prep. Time:

10 minutes

Cooking Time:

10 minutes

Cooling Time:

20 minutes or so

1. In a small saucepan, mix dry ingredients.

2. Add egg and stir well. Stir in vinegar and water.

3. Bring to boil, stirring constantly. Cool.

4. Mix with 1 cup sour cream.

5. Cover tightly and refrigerate until needed. Enough for 2-3 pounds of shredded cabbage/carrot mix.

Honey Vinaigrette

¼ cup honey
½ cup red wine vinegar
2 Tbsp. Worcestershire sauce
1 cup olive oil or salad oil
½ tsp. salt
1 tsp. ground black pepper

Makes:

1¾ cups

Prep. Time:

10 minutes

1. Whisk all ingredients together.

2. Cover tightly and store in refrigerator.

Balsamic Vinaigrette

¼ cup water
¼ cup balsamic vinegar
2 Tbsp. olive oil
1 Tbsp. Dijon mustard
1 Tbsp. dried basil
½ tsp. black pepper

Makes:
_____

½ cup

Prep. Time:
_____

10 minutes

Mix well, cover tightly, and store in refrigerator.

Hidden Valley Ranch Mix

5 Tbsp. dried minced onion

4 tsp. salt

7 tsp. dried parsley

1 tsp. garlic powder

Combine and store in an airtight container.

To make dressing:

Combine 2 Tbsp. mix with 1 cup mayonnaise and 1 cup sour cream.

To make dip:

Combine 2 Tbsp. mix with 2 cups sour cream.

Eat-N-House French Dressing

2 cups salad dressing (or use recipe on page 64)

1 cup sugar

½ cup apple cider vinegar

⅓ cup ketchup

1 onion, chopped fine

1 tsp. Worcestershire sauce

½ tsp. paprika

½ tsp. dry mustard

½ tsp. salt

½ tsp. pepper

⅓ cup oil

1. Combine all ingredients except oil and blend well.

2. Whisk in oil.

3. Cover and refrigerate.

Makes:

about 4 cups

Prep. Time:

10 minutes

Variation:

Add 2 Tbsp. taco seasoning when using in taco salad.

Italian Dressing

1½ cups olive oil
½ cup red wine vinegar
1 Tbsp. honey
1 clove garlic
¼ cup grated Parmesan cheese
minced fresh parsley

¼ tsp. paprika
¼ tsp. dried basil
½ tsp. dry mustard
½ tsp. celery salt
½ tsp. pepper

Makes:

about 2 cups

Prep. Time:

10 minutes

1. Combine in a blender.

2. Cover and blend until smooth.

3. Cover tightly and store in refrigerator.

Sweet and Sour Dressing

1 cup sugar
1 Tbsp. all-purpose flour
1 tsp. salt
1 egg
3 Tbsp. apple cider vinegar
1 Tbsp. butter, softened to room temperature
1 Tbsp. prepared mustard
1 Tbsp. water
3 Tbsp. salad dressing (or use recipe on page 64)
cream, optional

Makes:
about 1½ cups

Prep. Time:
10 minutes

Cooking Time:
10 minutes

Cooling Time:
1–2 hours

1. Set up double boiler to begin boiling.

2. Mix together sugar, flour, and salt in top of double boiler.

3. Whisk in egg, vinegar, butter, mustard, and water.

4. Cook in top of double boiler, stirring frequently.

5. When thick, remove from heat. Cool.

6. Add salad dressing. Thin with a little cream if desired.

The "FARM HOME" Cookbook

SOUPS, STEWS, *and* CHOWDERS

Fresh Corn Chowder

2 Tbsp. (¼ stick) butter
1 medium onion, chopped
1 rib celery, chopped
½ cup diced green bell
   pepper
2-3 red-skinned potatoes,
   cubed
3-4 Tbsp. all-purpose flour
½ tsp. dried basil
½ tsp. dried marjoram

2 cups chicken broth
2 cups corn, cut off from
   about 4 ears
1¼ cups milk
¾ cup heavy cream
salt and pepper to taste
bacon bits, for garnish,
   optional
fresh snipped parsley, for
   garnish, *optional*

Makes:

4-6 servings

Prep. Time:

15 minutes

Cooking Time:

35 minutes

1. In soup pot or Dutch oven, sauté onion in butter until soft.

2. Add celery, peppers, and potatoes. Cook 5 minutes, stirring periodically.

3. Stir in flour and cook 2 more minutes.

4. Add herbs and chicken broth. Stir until well blended.

5. Cover and simmer over low heat for 30 minutes, or until potatoes are tender.

6. Stir in corn, milk, cream, and salt and pepper to taste.

7. Reheat but do *not* allow to boil.

8. Stir in bacon bits and parsley if you wish.

Garlic Broth with Parsley Spaetzle

1 Tbsp. olive oil
3 *or* 4 heads garlic, cloves
    peeled, and chopped
8 cups vegetable *or* chicken
    stock
salt and pepper

Parsley spaetzle:
2 eggs, lightly beaten
1½ cups all-purpose flour
½ cup water
½ tsp. salt
½ tsp. black pepper
¼ tsp. baking powder
½ cup chopped parsley

To prepare the broth:

1. Heat oil in large saucepan over low heat. Stir in chopped garlic and sauté, stirring often, until garlic is soft and translucent, but **not** browned, about 20 minutes.

2. Add the stock and bring to a boil. Reduce heat and simmer, uncovered, for about 45 minutes or until garlic is very tender.

3. Season with salt and pepper. Keep warm.

4. Make spaetzle by combining all spaetzle ingredients in a bowl. Stir until dough forms.

5. Cover and refrigerate 1 hour.

6. Bring a pot of salted water to a boil.

7. Drop small bits of batter, about the size of a dime, into the boiling water from a spoon. Cook until the spaetzle is light and delicate, about 5 minutes. Drain.

8. To serve, add the spaetzle to the warm garlic broth.

Makes:

6-8 servings

Prep. Time:

30 minutes

Chilling Time:

1 hour

Cooking Time:

1 hour

Tip:

Our German friends who make spaetzle also serve it with sausage and coleslaw.

Swiss Onion Soup

6 Tbsp. (¾ stick) butter
3 large onions, chopped
1½ cups chicken broth
1 Tbsp. powdered chicken bouillon
¼ cup all-purpose flour
1¾ cup milk, *divided*
1½ cups shredded Swiss cheese, *divided*
pepper, to taste
2 cups croutons (see recipes on pages 95 and 96)
fresh minced chives *or* parsley

Makes:

3-4 servings

Prep. Time:

15 minutes

Cooking Time:

35 minutes

1. In a large saucepan, sauté onions in butter over medium heat until browned, about 15 minutes.

2. Stir in broth and chicken bouillon. Bring to boil.

3. Reduce heat. Cover and simmer for 15 minutes.

4. In a jar with a tight-fitting lid, combine flour and ½ cup milk. Shake until smooth. Gradually stir into onion mixture.

5. Stir in remaining milk. Bring to a boil, boiling for 2 minutes, stirring until thickened.

6. Reduce heat and stir in ¾ cup cheese and pepper. Taste and adjust salt.

7. Ladle into ovenproof bowls. Sprinkle with croutons and remaining cheese.

8. Broil 4" from heat until cheese is melted and bubbly.

9. Garnish with chives or parsley.

Creamy Tomato Basil Soup

4 cups canned tomato juice
1 tsp. salt
½ cup sugar
½ tsp. pepper
2 cups milk
3 Tbsp. all-purpose flour
1 Tbsp. dried basil *or* 3 Tbsp. fresh minced basil leaves

Makes:

6 servings

Prep. Time:

10 minutes

Cooking Time:

20 minutes

1. Heat tomato juice in saucepan.

2. Add salt, sugar, and pepper to juice.

3. Add flour to milk in a jar with a tight-fitting lid. Shake milk and flour until thoroughly blended.

4. Add to tomato juice.

5. Cook on low heat stirring with a spatula until it comes to a rolling boil. Boil for 2 minutes until mixture is smooth and creamy.

6. Sprinkle dried basil (or use fresh basil sprigs) over tomato mixture and fold in with spatula.

7. Adjust salt and pepper to taste.

I moved a planter of herbs onto the kitchen windowsill this fall. I often add a sprig here and there when I'm cooking. Even just brushing the herbs with my fingers gives off such a pleasant aroma.

Asparagus Soup

2 cups chicken broth
3 cups chopped asparagus
1 onion, chopped
3 Tbsp. butter
3 Tbsp. all-purpose flour
1 tsp. salt
pepper to taste
2¼ cups milk
1 cup shredded cheese
1–2 cups leftover mashed potatoes

Makes:

4 servings

Prep. Time:

10 minutes

Cooking Time:

30 minutes

1. Simmer chopped asparagus in chicken broth till tender but still crunchy. Set aside.

2. In another soup pot, sauté onion and butter.

3. Stir flour, salt, and pepper to taste into onions.

4. Add milk and cheese to onion mixture, cooking and stirring until cheese melts.

5. Add asparagus in chicken broth and leftover mashed potatoes to milk/cheese/onion mixture. The more mashed potatoes you add, the thicker the soup.

6. Heat through and serve.

Italian Vegetable Soup

1 lb. ground beef
2 cloves garlic, minced
1 cup diced onion
salt, to taste
2 cups water
5 tsp. beef bouillon
½ tsp. dried oregano
¼ tsp. pepper
½ tsp. dried basil
1 Tbsp. parsley
1 cup sliced celery
1 cup sliced carrots

2 cups canned whole
   tomatoes
2 cups tomato sauce
2 cups kidney beans, cooked,
   drained, rinsed
2 cups shredded cabbage
1 cup frozen green beans
½ cup uncooked macaroni,
   optional
¾ cup grated Parmesan
   cheese, for serving

Makes:

8–10 servings

Prep. Time:

30 minutes

Cooking Time:

35 minutes

1. In a soup pot, brown ground beef with garlic, onion and salt to taste. Drain off drippings.

2. Add water, bouillon, seasonings, celery, carrots, tomatoes, tomato sauce, and kidney beans.

3. Bring to a boil. Reduce heat and simmer 20 minutes.

4. Add cabbage, green beans, and macaroni if desired.

5. Simmer until all vegetables are tender, approximately 10 minutes.

6. Taste for salt. Add more herbs if desired.

7. Sprinkle with Parmesan cheese when serving.

Cream of Mushroom Soup

3 Tbsp. butter
1 cup finely chopped mushrooms
2 Tbsp. all-purpose flour
⅛ tsp. pepper
1 tsp. salt
1 cup milk
1 cup heavy cream
2 cups chicken broth
¼ tsp. paprika
½ tsp. onion salt

Makes:
4 servings

Prep. Time:
15 minutes

Cooking Time:
20 minutes

1. Melt butter over low heat in heavy saucepan. Add mushrooms.

2. Sauté for 5 or so minutes.

3. Blend in flour, pepper, and salt.

4. Remove from heat and stir in milk, cream, and chicken broth.

5. Bring to a boil and cook for 1 minute.

6. Add paprika and onion salt, and bring just to a boil.

While Cream of Mushroom Soup is often useful as an ingredient, it is also a delicious soup in its own right. Add some cooked noodles to the soup if you wish, and serve with cheese and crackers and a plate of fresh veggies for a delicious light lunch or supper.

Broccoli Chowder

2 Tbsp. (¼ stick) butter
⅔ cup diced green bell pepper
⅔ cup chopped onion
2 Tbsp. all-purpose flour
½ tsp. salt
2 cups milk
2 cups chicken broth
2 cups finely chopped broccoli, about half a head
1 cup shredded Swiss cheese

Makes:

4 servings

Prep. Time:

12 minutes

Cooking Time:

15 minutes

Variation:

Cheddar, longhorn, or other cheeses can be substituted for Swiss.

1. In a medium saucepan, melt butter.

2. Add green pepper and onion. Cook and stir occasionally until vegetables are crisp-tender, about 5 minutes.

3. Stir in flour and salt. Cook and stir for 1 minute.

4. Stir in milk, broth, and broccoli. Cook until mixture is smooth and thickened.

5. Stir in cheese. Cook and stir until cheese melts and mixture is hot, about 2 minutes.

Cream of Potato Soup with Sausage

2 Tbsp. (¼ stick) butter
½ lb. smoked sausage, sliced
    thinly
1 onion, chopped
1 Tbsp. all-purpose flour
4 cups milk

2 cups cooked minced *or*
    riced potatoes
1½ tsp. salt
¼ tsp. pepper
snipped fresh parsley, for
    garnish

Makes:

4 servings

Prep. Time:

10 minutes

Cooking Time:

20 minutes

1. In soup pot, melt butter. Add sausage slices and onions.

2. Cook two minutes. Push sausage and onions to one side and add flour.

3. When flour is well blended into drippings, add milk gradually, stirring.

4. Then add potatoes and seasonings. Cook until thickened and serve.

Hearty Ham Soup

1½ cups diced potatoes
1 cup diced carrots
½ cup chopped celery
1 small onion, chopped
1½ tsp. powdered chicken bouillon
¼ cup (half stick) butter
1½ cups diced cooked ham
4 cups milk
2 Tbsp. cornstarch
¼ cup water
1 cup shredded cheddar cheese

1. Put vegetables in soup pot with water just barely covering them. Bring to a boil and cook 5 minutes.

2. Add chicken bouillon and butter. Cook until vegetables are tender.

3. Add ham and milk. Bring to a boil.

4. Make a paste of cornstarch and water to thicken. Stir into soup.

5. Bring to a boil then add cheese.

6. Heat until very hot, but do not boil after cheese is added.

Makes:

6-8 servings

Prep Time:

20 minutes

Cooking Time:

35-40 minutes

Variation:

I usually cook the vegetables in chicken broth instead of the water and chicken base. I also like to add some sprigs of parsley.

Brown Bean and Ham Soup

1 lb. dry pinto beans

10 cups water

2 cups diced ham, *or* a ham bone with a generous amount of meat on it

½ tsp. salt

¼ tsp. black pepper

1. Wash beans. Place them in a soup pot with 10 cups fresh water.

2. Bring to a boil, reduce the heat, and simmer 3 minutes. Remove from heat, cover and let stand for 1 hour.

3. Then add the ham or ham bone and seasonings and return to the stove.

4. Bring to a boil, reduce the heat, and simmer for 1½ to 2 hours or until the beans are tender but not mushy.

5. Remove the ham bone and cut off the meat. Dice meat and return to the soup.

Makes:

6–8 servings

Prep. Time:

15 minutes

Standing Time:

1 hour

Cooking Time:

2–3 hours

Variation:

Brown Dutch or Painted Pony beans can also be used. Dry beans can also be soaked in cold water overnight, cutting way back on cooking time.

Reuben Soup

7½ cups chicken broth
1 lb. cooked bulk sausage *or* sliced links
4-6 cups shredded cabbage
½ cup chopped onion
2 cups uncooked whole grain spaghetti
¼ tsp. garlic powder
salt and pepper, to taste
1 cup shredded Swiss cheese

Makes:

4-6 servings

Prep. Time:

15 minutes

Cooking Time:

15 minutes

1. In a soup pot, combine all ingredients except cheese.

2. Bring to a boil, then simmer for 15 minutes, or until cabbage and pasta are soft.

3. Add salt and pepper as desired.

4. Garnish with cheese and serve.

Big Batch Hearty Ham Soup

6 quarts cubed potatoes
2 large onions, diced
2 quarts diced celery
2 quarts carrots, diced
2 cups (4 sticks) butter
3 cups all-purpose flour

2½-3 gallons milk, *divided*
6 lbs. cooked ham chunks
pepper, to taste
salt, to taste
2 lbs. cheese, any variety, grated

Makes:

24 quarts

Prep. Time:

depends on the number of helpers and gadgets

Cooking Time:

1-2 hours

1. Cook each vegetable separately until tender. Drain each and set aside.

2. Melt butter in large stockpot. Add flour. Stir over heat until browned.

3. Add 1 gallon milk. Heat until almost boiling.

4. Add ham, vegetables, and remaining milk.

5. Heat through, then add cheese. Stir until melted. Adjust seasonings. Do not boil.

This is a good soup to make on a family workday, then each can take a meal along home. Local hardware stores with good housewares sections have many handy gadgets to slice and dice, cutting preparation time drastically.

Workdays can be organized by family, women, or neighbors. I get together one day every month with my girls (daughters and daughters-in-law), taking turns at each others' homes. Wherever we congregate, we do whatever that person wants us to do.

We do a wide range of things. We were at daughter Ann's in May, and she had us mulch her flowerbeds. In April we were at Martha's and it was cold, so we worked inside. Some cleaned her cupboards, I cracked hickory nuts, and then helped tear/cut carpet rags, sewed them together and rolled into balls. She will then take them to one of our carpet makers in the area and have them made into carpets. Here in June it's my turn, and I haven't fully decided what I'll have them do.

Of course, we have coffee and cookies and sit around the table chatting for a while before someone says, "We'd better get at it" and the pieces fly! We get a lot done in a day, and it is fun! The day starts around 8:30, and since everyone has chores to do, we usually head for home around 3:00.

I should mention that whoever hosts the workday does no cooking; the others bring the food. Since the hubbies are all farmers, they often end up coming for dinner, too.

Then there are days when someone just needs some help unexpectedly, so we go to help. In the fall, everyone comes home to our farm for a day to help cut firewood for the winter.

Working with food is also common—butchering chickens, freezing a big batch of corn, getting apples ready for drying, etc. It's a great system. Very enjoyable, too!

Harvest Stew

2 Tbsp. (¼ stick) butter
1½ lbs. boneless pork, cut in
    cubes
1 medium onion, chopped
3 cups chicken broth
2 bay leaves
¼ tsp. rosemary

¼ tsp. sage
pinch of pepper
1 medium butternut squash,
    peeled and cut in cubes
2 medium apples, peeled and
    chopped
salt, to taste

Makes:

4-6 servings

Prep. Time:

25 minutes

Cooking Time:

50 minutes

1. Melt butter in soup pot.

2. Add pork and onion. Sauté until meat is no longer pink.

3. Add chicken broth, bay leaves, rosemary, sage, and pepper.

4. Cover and bring to a boil.

5. Add squash and apples. Simmer uncovered until squash and apples are tender, about 20 minutes.

6. Taste for salt. Remove bay leaves before serving.

Creamy White Chili

1 lb. boneless chicken
    breasts, cubed
1 medium onion, chopped
2 cloves garlic, minced
1 Tbsp. butter
2 pints (32 ozs.) cannellini
    or great northern beans,
    drained and rinsed
2 cups chicken broth

1 cup chopped green chilies,
    or home-canned hot
    peppers
1 tsp. salt
1 tsp. ground cumin, *optional*
1 tsp. dried oregano
½ tsp. pepper
1 cup sour cream
1 cup heavy whipping cream

Makes:

4-6 servings

Prep. Time:

20 minutes

Cooking Time:

45 minutes

1. In large saucepan, sauté chicken, onion, and garlic in butter until chicken is partially cooked.

2. Add drained beans, chicken broth, chilies, and seasonings.

3. Bring to a boil. Reduce heat; simmer uncovered for 30 minutes.

4. Last, add the sour cream and whipping cream.

5. Heat, but do *not* boil.

Tip:

If too thick, some milk can be added. Start with 2 cups dry beans if you wish to cook your own.

Lazy Day Stew

2 lbs. stew meat, *or* any cut of beef, cut in chunks
1 cup sliced carrots
3-4 potatoes, cut up
1½ cups green beans, cut in 1" lengths
1 tsp. salt
pepper, to taste
1 onion, sliced
1¼ cups cream of mushroom soup (see recipe on page 81 to make your own)
⅓ cup water

Makes:

6-8 servings

Prep. Time:

15 minutes

Baking Time:

4-5 hours

1. Combine all ingredients in a 2-quart baking dish with lid. (Everything is put together raw.)

2. Cover. Bake 4 hours at 300°, *or* 5 hours at 275°.

This was a favorite when our family was growing up, and a great hit with Mom. So convenient.

Cabbage Borscht

2-lb. beef soup bone with
    lots of meat
8 cups water
2-4 carrots, sliced
4 medium potatoes, cubed
1 large onion, chopped
1 medium head cabbage,
    chopped
handful of fresh dill

2 whole dried chili peppers
2 cups chopped tomatoes,
    optional
2½ cups tomato soup *or*
    pureed tomatoes
¼ tsp. pepper
2 tsp. salt
sour cream, for serving

Makes:

12-15 servings

Prep. Time:

30 minutes

Cooking Time:

2½ hours

1. Cover soup bone with water and simmer for several hours until meat is tender.

2. Remove the bone and shred the meat. Set aside.

3. Add more water to measure a total of 8-10 cups stock. Add carrots, potatoes, onions, and cabbage to the pot.

4. Place dill and chili peppers into a spice holder or cheesecloth that you tie shut. Drop into the soup pot. Cook until vegetables are tender.

5. Add chopped tomatoes, tomato soup, and shredded beef. Bring to a boil.

6. Remove chili peppers and dill before serving.

7. Serve with a dollop of sour cream on each filled soup bowl.

Taco Soup

2 lbs. ground beef

1 small onion

2 Tbsp. taco seasoning (see recipe for MIY Taco Seasoning on page 271)

¼ cup sugar

2 16-oz. cans pork & beans

4 cups whole-kernel corn

2 quarts (8 cups) tomato juice

crushed tortilla chips, for serving

shredded cheddar cheese, for serving

sour cream, for serving

shredded lettuce, for serving

Makes:

6-8 servings

Prep. Time:

15 minutes

Cooking Time:

35 minutes

1. Brown the ground beef and onion in a good-sized soup pot.

2. Add taco seasoning, sugar, pork and beans, corn, and tomato juice.

3. Bring to a boil, then simmer for 15-30 minutes. Taste for salt and add if needed.

4. Serve over crushed tortilla chips.

5. Sprinkle cheddar cheese over top.

6. Add sour cream and lettuce.

This is good over an open fire, for a cookout or camping.

Foggy Day Chili

2 Tbsp. olive oil
1 medium onion, diced
1 Tbsp. minced garlic
1½ lbs. ground beef
1 Tbsp. ground cumin
1 Tbsp. chili powder
2 tsp. dried oregano
2 cups cooked black beans with cooking liquid
2 cups cooked cannellini beans with cooking liquid
1 quart tomato juice
1 tsp. salt, *or* more to taste
black pepper
red pepper flakes, to taste
grated cheese, for serving
sour cream, for serving

1. Heat oil in heavy soup pot. Add onion and cook for 5 minutes.

2. Add garlic and cook for one minute longer.

3. Add beef, breaking up meat with a wooden spoon.

4. Add cumin, chili powder, and oregano.

5. Cook, stirring frequently until meat is browned.

6. Add beans and tomato juice. Bring chili to a boil.

7. Reduce heat to low, cover pot, and let chili simmer, stirring occasionally until thickened, about 45 minutes.

8. Add salt, then taste for seasoning and add more salt as needed, along with black pepper, and red pepper flakes if desired.

9. Serve chili topped with grated cheese and sour cream.

Makes:

10 servings

Prep. Time:

15 minutes

Cooking Time:

60–70 minutes

Note:

Good served with cornbread.

Variation:

If you don't have your own canned beans and tomatoes, use 15-oz. cans of beans and 28-oz. can of diced tomatoes. Don't drain them.

Hearty Hamburger Vegetable Soup

2 Tbsp. (¼ stick) butter
1 lb. ground beef
½ cup diced onion
1 cup diced potatoes
1 cup diced carrots
½ cup diced celery

2 cups tomato juice
1½ tsp. salt
1 tsp. seasoned salt
½ tsp. pepper
¼ cup flour
4 cups milk

Makes:

6–8 servings

Prep. Time:

30 minutes

Cooking Time:

40 minutes

Variation:

Very good served over rice!

1. Melt butter in soup pot. Brown beef and onion in butter.

2. Stir in potatoes, carrots, celery, tomato juice, salt, seasoned salt, and pepper.

3. Cook, covered, until vegetables are tender.

4. Separately, add flour to milk and whisk until smooth. Then stir into vegetable mixture.

5. Stir until thickened.

This is only the second year I've planted leeks. I plan to mulch the plants with straw and hope I can use them all winter long. Leeks make a wonderful creamy soup. They're milder than onions, but very flavorful.

Herbed Croutons

½ cup (1 stick) butter
¼ cup grated Parmesan cheese
1 tsp. salt
1½ tsp. dried oregano
1½ tsp. parsley flakes
1½ tsp. celery seed
1½ tsp. garlic powder
1 Tbsp. dried basil
1 Tbsp. onion powder
8-10 cups cubed bread, about 1 small loaf

Makes:

8-10 cups

Prep. Time:

10 minutes

Baking Time:

4 hours

1. Melt butter, then add Parmesan and seasonings.

2. Pour over cubed bread and toss.

3. Spread onto baking sheet and put in oven set at lowest temperature, ideally 150°. Bake until dry, about 4 hours. (If you can't set your oven that low, you may need to shorten the baking time.)

4. Serve in soup or on salad.

When I have crusts and crumbled pieces of bread that aren't getting used, I put them into the freezer until I have enough to make a batch of these croutons.

Quick Croutons

½ cup (1 stick) butter
1½ tsp. garlic salt
3 cups bread cubes

1. Put butter into skillet and melt. Add garlic salt.

2. Add bread cubes and toss over medium heat until golden brown.

3. Remove from skillet and allow to fully cool.

4. Great in soup or on salad.

Makes:

3 cups

Prep. Time:

5 minutes

Cooking Time:

5-10 minutes

Parsley Cubes

1½-2 cups chopped fresh parsley
1 Tbsp. canola or olive oil

1. Add oil to chopped parsley and blend briefly in blender.

2. Spoon into ice cube trays to freeze.

3. When frozen, remove parsley cubes and place in sealed containers. The oil keeps cubes from getting frosty and makes them easier to remove from the tray.

Makes:

6-8 cubes

Prep. Time:

5 minutes

Freezing Time:

a few hours

Great for adding some fresh seasoning to soups and stews in the winter when you do not have fresh parsley.

The "Farm Home" Cookbook

MEATS and MAIN DISHES

Sirloin Stir Fry

4 Tbsp. (half stick) butter, *divided*
1 cup chopped broccoli
1 cup chopped onion
1 cup sliced summer squash
2 cups shredded cabbage
salt and pepper, to taste
1½ lbs. sirloin steak, sliced in ½" strips
2–3 Tbsp. soy sauce
1 cup beef broth
2 Tbsp. cornstarch
1 cup water
cooked brown rice, for serving

Makes:

6 servings

Prep. Time:

25 minutes

Cooking time:

15 minutes

1. Melt 2 Tbsp. butter in large skillet.

2. Stir fry vegetables for 5 minutes, adding salt and pepper as desired. Remove from skillet and set aside.

3. Add 2 Tbsp. butter to skillet. Brown meat strips on both sides until no pinkness remains.

4. Add soy sauce and broth to meat. While this comes to a boil, mix cornstarch into water until smooth.

5. Add cornstarch water to boiling meat mixture, stirring until smooth and slightly thickened.

6. Stir vegetables into meat mixture, bring to boiling again and turn off heat.

7. Serve over hot brown rice.

We eat a lot of stir fry during the summer with all the fresh vegetables. Later in the summer, when green and red peppers are ready in the garden, we use sliced pepper strips as the main vegetables in this stir fry.

Oven Barbecued Steaks

3-lb. round steak, cut ¾" thick
2 Tbsp. (¼ stick) butter
½ cup chopped onion
¾ cup ketchup
½ cup apple cider vinegar
¾ cup water
1 Tbsp. brown sugar
1 tsp. prepared mustard
1 Tbsp. Worcestershire sauce
1 tsp. salt
½ tsp. black pepper

Makes:

10 servings

Prep. Time:

30 minutes

Cooking/Baking
Time:

2½ hours

1. Preheat oven to 350°.

2. Cut steak into 10 equal portions.

3. Put butter in skillet. Brown each piece of steak on both sides, being careful not to crowd the pan so the meat browns, rather than steaming in its own juice.

4. Transfer steaks to a roasting pan.

5. Add onions to butter and drippings in skillet and brown lightly.

6. Add the rest of the ingredients to skillet to make a barbecue sauce. Simmer 5 minutes.

7. Pour sauce over steaks in pan. Cover.

8. Bake for 2 hours or more until meat is fork-tender.

Meatloaf Pie

1 lb. ground beef
½ cup fresh bread crumbs
½ cup tomato sauce
¼ cup chopped onions
¼ cup chopped green bell pepper
¼ tsp. dried oregano
1½ tsp. salt
freshly ground pepper to taste
1⅓ cups instant rice
1 cup water
1½ cups tomato sauce
½ tsp. salt
1 cup grated sharp cheddar cheese, *divided*

Makes:

6 servings

Prep. Time:

20 minutes

Baking Time:

40–45 minutes

1. Preheat oven to 350°.

2. Mix ground beef, bread crumbs, tomato sauce, onions, green pepper, oregano, salt, and pepper together.

3. Pat into a greased 9" pie plate to form a shell with a 1" fluting around the edge.

4. Combine rice, water, tomato sauce, and ¼ cup of the cheese.

5. Fill meat shell with rice mixture and cover with foil.

6. Bake in preheated oven for 25 minutes.

7. Uncover and sprinkle with remaining ¾ cup cheese.

8. Continue to bake, uncovered, another 10–15 minutes, until rice is tender.

Cheeseburger Pizza

⅔ cup ketchup

1 Tbsp. prepared mustard

12" unbaked pizza crust (see recipe on page 38)

2 cups shredded cheese

1 lb. ground beef, browned and drained

1 tsp. salt

¼ tsp. pepper

½ cup real bacon bits

small onion, diced

½ cup diced dill pickles

shredded lettuce

chopped tomatoes

Makes:

4 servings

Prep. Time:

15 minutes

Baking Time:

10 minutes

1. Preheat oven to 450°.

2. In a small bowl, mix ketchup and mustard together. Spread over pizza crust. Top with cheese.

3. Add salt and pepper to browned beef. Sprinkle beef and bacon on top of cheese.

4. Bake in preheated oven for 10 minutes.

5. Top individual pizza slices with lettuce and tomatoes at the table.

Grilled Herbed Burgers

1 lb. ground beef
1 egg, beaten
2 Tbsp. dry bread crumbs
¼ cup chopped onion
1 clove garlic, minced
2 Tbsp. snipped fresh basil
whole wheat bread, butter, for serving
lettuce, tomato, spinach, fresh basil, for serving

Makes:

4 servings

Prep. Time:

10 minutes

Grilling Time:

20-25 minutes

1. Combine beef, egg, bread crumbs, onion, garlic, and snipped basil.

2. Shape into four patties.

3. Grill for 15-20 minutes, turning once halfway through grilling.

4. Serve on toasted whole wheat bread spread with butter. Top with lettuce, tomato slices, fresh spinach leaves, and fresh basil leaves.

Grilled Pineapple Burgers

2 lbs. ground beef
1 tsp. salt
¼ cup brown sugar
¼ cup honey
15-oz. can pineapple slices, drained
8 slices bacon
3 Tbsp. Italian salad dressing (see recipe on page 71)
¾ cup barbecue sauce, plus more for grilling (see recipe on page 129)
⅛ tsp. pepper
1 Tbsp. lemon juice

Makes:

8 servings

Prep. Time:

20 minutes

Marinating Time:

2 hours

Grilling Time:

15-20 minutes

1. In a mixing bowl, mix beef, salt, brown sugar, and honey together. Shape into 8 patties.

2. Press pineapple slice onto each patty.

3. Wrap each patty with a bacon slice. Secure with a toothpick.

4. In a bowl, mix Italian dressing, barbecue sauce, pepper, and lemon juice together.

5. Place the burgers in a glass baking dish.

6. Pour all the sauce over the burgers.

7. Cover and refrigerate for at least 2 hours.

8. Grill the burgers for 15-20 minutes, until cooked to your preference. Baste with barbecue sauce during grilling.

After a late start because of the late spring, the garden is doing well. Some early tomatoes are blooming, and I visualize red, juicy slices on a grilled hamburger.

Sloppy Joes

2 lbs. ground beef
½ cup chopped onions
1 tsp. salt
1 tsp. pepper
3 Tbsp. all-purpose flour
1 Tbsp. Worcestershire sauce
1 cup tomato sauce
2 cups ketchup
2 Tbsp. brown sugar
2 Tbsp. prepared mustard
1 tsp. garlic salt
buns, for serving

Makes:

8-10 servings

Prep. Time:

15 minutes

Cooking Time:

1 hour

1. Mix together ground beef, onions, salt, and pepper in a Dutch oven.

2. Brown slightly. Sprinkle flour over all. Mix well and brown briefly.

3. Add all remaining ingredients. Simmer uncovered 1 hour or longer, stirring every 15 minutes.

4. Serve hot, on buns.

Italian Meatballs

1 cup dry bread crumbs
½ cup milk
¾ cup grated Parmesan
  cheese
½ cup chopped fresh parsley
3 eggs, beaten
2 Tbsp. dried oregano
2 tsp. dried basil

1 Tbsp. minced garlic
1 Tbsp. salt
1 Tbsp. pepper
1 tsp. crushed red pepper
  flakes
pinch of nutmeg
1½ cups beef broth, *divided*
2 lbs. ground beef

Makes:

30 meatballs

Prep. Time:

20 minutes

Baking Time:

25 minutes

1. In a large mixing bowl, stir together all ingredients except ground beef and beef broth. Mix thoroughly.

2. Add ground beef and ½ cup broth. Mix thoroughly again.

3. Preheat oven to 350°.

4. Shape ground beef mixture into 2" balls.

5. Space meatballs on greased rimmed baking sheet cookie sheet so they're not touching.

6. Add remaining 1 cup beef broth to bottom of pan (this keeps the meatballs juicy).

7. Bake for 25 minutes preheated oven, or until meatballs are just cooked through.

Meatball Vegetable Skillet

1 lb. ground beef
½ cup dry bread crumbs
½ cup tomato juice
1 egg
2 Tbsp. minced onion
1 tsp. Worcestershire sauce
1 tsp. salt
¼ tsp. pepper
2-4 Tbsp. all-purpose flour
2 Tbsp. lard
2 cups diced potatoes
2 cups frozen peas
4 carrots, sliced
1 cup water
salt and pepper, to taste

Makes:

5-6 servings

Prep. Time:

20 minutes

Cooking Time:

40 minutes

1. Make meatballs by mixing ground beef, bread crumbs, tomato juice, egg, onion, Worcestershire sauce, salt, and pepper together in a large bowl.

2. Form into 1" balls.

3. Roll meatballs in flour.

4. Melt lard in skillet. Add meatballs and brown on all sides. Do in batches, rather than crowd the skillet, so the meatballs brown rather than steam in their own juices.

5. Place cooked meatballs in Dutch oven. Add vegetables and water. Sprinkle with salt and pepper to taste.

6. Cook covered on low for 30 minutes until vegetables are tender and meatballs are cooked through.

Barbecued Venison Meatballs

3 lbs. ground venison
1 cup dry quick oats
2 eggs
½ tsp. garlic powder
12-oz. can evaporated milk
1 cup cracker crumbs
½ cup chopped onions
2 tsp. chili powder

Sauce
2 cups ketchup
½ tsp. garlic powder
1 cup brown sugar
¼ cup chopped onions
½ tsp. liquid smoke

Makes:

12–15 servings

Prep. Time:

15 minutes

Baking Time:

1 hour

1. Preheat oven to 350°.

2. Combine all meatball ingredients in mixing bowl. Mixture will be soft.

3. Shape into walnut-sized balls, and put in greased baking pan in single layer.

4. Mix sauce ingredients together, stirring until sugar dissolves.

5. Pour sauce over balls. Bake in preheated oven for 1 hour.

Unbaked meatballs can be put in a single layer on waxed-paper-lined baking sheets and frozen until solid, then put into bags to use when desired. When you're ready to use them, add sauce and bake for an extra 15 minutes.

Curry and Rice with Chop Salad

2 cups brown rice
4 cups water
1 tsp. salt
2 lbs. ground beef
salt and pepper, to taste
1 Tbsp. curry powder
2 Tbsp. maple syrup
1 Tbsp. flour
2 cups tomato juice *or* tomato sauce

Chop Salad

2 cups fresh tomatoes, cut up in chunks
1 cup chopped green bell pepper
1 onion, chopped coarsely
¾ cup apple cider vinegar
½ cup water
½ cup sugar *or* honey

Makes:

8–10 servings

Prep. Time:

20 minutes

Cooking Time:

55 minutes

1. Put 2 cups brown rice in saucepan. Add water and 1 tsp. salt. Bring to a boil and simmer, covered, for 45–60 minutes, until water is absorbed and rice is tender.

This is one of our family favorites.

2. While rice is cooking, brown ground beef in Dutch oven.

3. Add salt and pepper to taste. Add curry powder and maple syrup.

4. When beef is browned, sprinkle with flour. Blend well, then add tomato juice or sauce. Heat through.

5. Make Chop Salad by combining tomatoes, green pepper, and onion in glass serving dish.

6. Blend vinegar, water, and sugar or honey. Pour over vegetables and mix gently.

7. To serve: each person puts rice on plate, next some curried ground beef, and chop salad on top.

Grilled Honey Garlic Pork Chops

¼ cup lemon juice
2 cloves garlic, minced
¼ cup honey

3 Tbsp. soy sauce
4 bone-in, ¾-1"-thick pork
chops

Makes:

Serves 4

Prep. Time:

10 minutes

Marinating Time:

at least 4 hours

Grilling Time:

10 minutes

1. Combine all ingredients except pork chops in a small bowl.

2. Place chops in a shallow dish. Cover with marinade and refrigerate at least 4 hours.

3. Remove chops from marinade.

4. Heat remaining marinade to boiling.

5. Grill pork chops over medium-hot coals for approximately 10 minutes, turning once during grilling. Baste frequently with cooked marinade. Grill just until an instant-read meat thermometer registers 145° (for rare) to 160° (for well-done) when inserted into the center of the chops without touching any bone.

German Pork Chops

3 large potatoes, sliced
¼ cup sliced onion, *optional*
salt, pepper, and caraway seeds, to taste
2 cups sauerkraut with juice
6 bone-in, ¾-1"-thick pork chops

Makes:

6 servings

Prep. Time:

15 minutes

Baking Time:

1 hour

1. Place potatoes, and onion if you wish, in bottom of greased 9" × 9" baking dish, or equivalent.

2. Season with salt, pepper, and caraway seed.

3. Preheat oven to 350°.

4. Drain sauerkraut, reserving ⅓ cup juice.

5. Place sauerkraut on top of potatoes.

6. Place chops on top of sauerkraut.

7. Sprinkle with salt, pepper, and caraway seed again.

8. Pour reserved sauerkraut juice down along the side of the baking dish so as not to disturb the seasonings.

9. Bake, covered, in preheated oven for one hour (juices should run clear), or until an instant-read meat thermometer registers 145° (for rare) to 160° (for well-done) when inserted into the center of the chops, without touching any bone. Uncover during last 15 minutes to brown chops.

Roast Pork with Apples and Pears

1 Tbsp. olive oil
2 apples, peeled or not, and thinly sliced
2 pears, peeled or not, and thinly sliced
salt and pepper, to taste
1 Tbsp. fresh sage, *divided*
1 Tbsp. fresh thyme, *divided*
1 tsp. fresh rosemary, *divided*
4 bone-in pork chops, ¾-1" thick
½ cup apple cider

Makes:

4 servings

Prep. Time:

10 minutes

Baking Time:

25 minutes

1. Use oil to grease a 9" × 9" baking dish. Place the apple and pear slices in dish and season with salt and half the chopped sage, thyme, and rosemary.

2. Preheat oven to 400°.

3. Place the pork chops on top of the fruit, sprinkle with salt, pepper, and the remaining herbs.

4. Spoon cider over top, being careful not to wash off the seasonings.

5. Bake at 400° for 15 minutes. Baste. Add more cider if the pan is drying out.

6. Roast for 5-10 additional minutes, or until an instant-read meat thermometer registers 145° (for rare) to 160°(for well-done) when inserted into the center of the chops without touching any bone. The apples and pears should be soft.

7. Serve the chops hot with the apple-pear sauce and any juices poured on top.

Cheesy Sausage Penne

1 lb. bulk sausage

1 garlic clove, minced

2½ cups spaghetti sauce

1 lb. dry penne pasta

8 oz. cream cheese, room temperature

1 cup sour cream

4 scallions, sliced

2 cups shredded cheddar cheese, *divided*

Makes:

6-8 servings

Prep. Time:

25 minutes

Cooking Time:

40 minutes

Baking Time:

35 minutes

1. In a large skillet cook the sausage and garlic over medium heat until meat is no longer pink. Drain off drippings.

2. Stir in spaghetti sauce. Bring to a boil. Reduce heat and simmer 20 minutes.

3. In a separate pan, cook penne according to package directions. Drain.

4. Combine penne and sauce.

5. Preheat oven to 350°.

6. In a small bowl, combine cream cheese, sour cream, and scallions.

7. In a greased, shallow, 3-quart baking dish, layer in half the pasta and sausage mixture.

8. Dollop with half the cream cheese mixture, then sprinkle with half the shredded cheese.

9. Repeat layers.

10. Bake uncovered in preheated oven for 30-35 minutes.

Butchering Day Scrapple

20 lbs. cornmeal
16 cups all-purpose flour
4 cups salt
¾–1 cup black pepper
1 Tbsp. red pepper

16 gallons broth, *or* broth and water, *divided*
1 qt. lard
4 gallons cooked, ground meat (butchering scraps)

Makes:

enough for 2-4 families

Prep. Time:

many hands make light work

Cooking Time:

about 2 hours

Chilling Time:

12 hours or more

Variation:

Add up to twice as much meat. Add salt and pepper according to your taste.

1. Divide cornmeal, flour, and seasonings into two food-grade 5-gallon buckets.

2. Add some measured broth and water to the cornmeal mixture to make a thick paste.

3. Bring the rest of the broth/water mixture to a boil in a large kettle. (We do this in a kettle outside over a fire.)

4. Then stir in the cornmeal mixture and lard.

5. Bring to a boil, stirring constantly for 45 minutes after it starts boiling again. If you have a hot fire under it and it is boiling down, you will need to add more water.

6. Add the cooked, ground meat. Cook for 15 more minutes. Keep stirring! (Between Steps 5 and 6, you will be cooking and stirring for an hour total.)

7. When the hour is up, use a large dipper to dip the scrapple mixture out of the kettle and into meat or bread pans.

8. Cover pans. Chill at least 12 hours until scrapple is firmly set. You may also freeze scrapple, either in blocks or slices.

9. To serve, slice into ¼-½"-thick slices. Dust with flour, and fry in half butter, half lard, until golden and crispy. Drain on paper towels. Serve with maple syrup on top, fried eggs beside, and cold milk to drink (our favorite), or with chicken gravy (my dad's favorite), or with apple butter (my friend's favorite). Whatever your family likes best!

Butchering time is a family or a neighborhood affair. Usually two to four families are involved; hence the huge recipe. It usually occurs during the coldest part of winter—in many cases around New Year's Day.

By the crack of dawn, the men start dressing the hogs, usually one per family, but it can be divided any way they want to. The women often arrive a bit later, and though they usually are not involved with the dressing, they are involved in every other aspect of the day's work: getting the meat ready for making sausage, grinding the cooked meat to put into the scrapple, and readying the fat to be rendered into lard in a big iron kettle over an open fire.

Tables are set up in a shop or outbuilding for stuffing sausage, cutting chops, and trimming all the meat off the bones. Today, instead of making such huge batches of scrapple (or panhaas, as many people call it), the meat and broth are often canned, allowing families to make a pan of scrapple whenever needed through the rest of the winter season.

Creamed Ham and Asparagus

1 lb. fresh asparagus
1 Tbsp. cornstarch
1½ cups milk, *divided*
2 Tbsp. (¼ stick) butter
1 tsp. salt
¼ tsp. pepper

2 Tbsp. fresh snipped parsley
1½ lbs. cooked ham, cubed
2 hard-boiled eggs, chopped
1 cup shredded cheddar
    cheese
toast or biscuits, for serving

Makes:

6–8 servings

Prep Time:

20 minutes

Cooking Time:

20 minutes

1. Cut asparagus into 1-inch pieces.

2. In a saucepan, cook asparagus in a small amount of water until crispy tender, about 5 minutes. Drain. Set asparagus aside.

3. In a saucepan, mix cornstarch and 2 Tbsp. milk until smooth. Add butter, salt, pepper, and remaining milk.

4. Cook and stir over medium heat until thickened and bubbly.

5. Add parsley, ham, eggs, cheese, and asparagus.

6. Cook over low heat and stir until ham is warmed and cheese is melted.

7. Serve on toast or over biscuits.

Chicken Thighs with Roasted Red Potato Crust

8 chicken thighs, bone in, skin on
salt and pepper to taste
4 Tbsp. extra-virgin olive oil, *divided*
4 cloves garlic, smashed, + 3 cloves garlic, slivered
⅓ cup balsamic vinegar
½ cup chicken broth
1½ Tbsp. chopped fresh rosemary
3-4 large red potatoes, cut in ¼" slices

Makes:

8 servings

Prep. Time:

15 minutes

Cooking Time:

20 minutes

Baking Time:

45 minutes

1. Season the chicken thighs with salt and pepper.

2. Heat 2 Tbsp. olive oil in a heavy, ovenproof skillet over medium-high heat. Brown the chicken pieces on both sides.

3. Remove chicken from skillet and drain on a paper towel.

4. Keep 1 Tbsp. oil/fat in the skillet and discard the rest. Turn heat to medium-high.

5. Add smashed garlic and vinegar, scraping the bottom to loosen any browned bits.

6. Add broth and rosemary and let boil, uncovered, until liquid is reduced by half.

7. Return chicken to skillet, cover, and lower heat. Simmer for 10 minutes.

8. Preheat oven to 400°.

9. In a large bowl, toss potato slices with garlic slivers, remaining 2 Tbsp. oil, and salt and pepper to taste.

10. Layer potato slices over the top of chicken, all the way to the edges.

11. Bake uncovered for 45 minutes in preheated oven, or until potato crust is golden brown. Spoon some of the pan juices over the chicken and potatoes with each serving.

Homestyle Shake and Bake Chicken

1½ cups all-purpose flour
1¼ tsp. dry mustard
3 tsp. salt
¾ tsp. black pepper

2 tsp. paprika
½ cup (1 stick) butter
3 lbs. chicken pieces

Makes:

6 servings

Prep. Time:

20 minutes

Baking Time:

1½ hours

1. Mix dry ingredients in shallow bowl. Set aside.

2. Melt butter in shallow saucepan.

3. Preheat oven to 350°. Cover baking sheet with aluminum foil.

4. Roll chicken in butter, then in dry mixture.

5. Place chicken in single layer on baking sheet.

6. Bake in preheated oven for 1½ hours, flipping pieces halfway through baking time to brown both sides.

Chicken Chipotle

Marinade for chicken:
2 Tbsp. lemon juice
1½ tsp. Lawry's salt
1½ tsp. dried oregano
1½ tsp. cumin
1 tsp. garlic salt
½ tsp. chili powder
½ tsp. paprika

1½ lbs. chicken breast, cut in 1½" pieces
2 Tbsp. (¼ stick) butter
2 cups white rice
1 cup chopped onions
2 Tbsp. olive oil
½ tsp. pepper
1½ tsp. salt, *divided*

4 tsp. powdered chicken bouillon
2½ tsp. cumin, *divided*
1 tsp. dried oregano
1 tsp. garlic powder
3½ cups water
2 cups black beans, drained
1½ tsp. chili powder
¾ tsp. lemon pepper
2-3 Tbsp. fresh chopped cilantro
2 cups sour cream
2-3 cups shredded cheddar cheese
chopped lettuce, salsa, and ranch dressing, for serving

Makes:

8-10 servings

Prep. Time:

20 minutes

Marinating Time:

overnight

Cooking Time:

40 minutes

Baking Time:

30 minutes

1. Marinate chicken overnight in marinade in refrigerator. Then brown in butter for 8-10 minutes, or grill. Set aside.

2. In a saucepan, sauté rice and onions in olive oil.

3. Add pepper, 1 tsp. salt, chicken bouillon, 1 tsp. cumin, oregano, garlic powder and water. Simmer, covered, for 20 minutes or until water is absorbed and rice is tender.

4. Preheat oven to 350°.

5. In a bowl, mix together beans, chili powder, ½ tsp. salt, 1½ tsp. cumin, lemon pepper, and cilantro.

6. Layer in 9" × 13" baking pan in this order: cooked rice, bean mixture, browned chicken, sour cream, and cheddar cheese.

7. Bake in preheated oven for 30 minutes.

8. Serve with lettuce, salsa, and ranch dressing.

Snow Peas and Chicken Skillet

2 Tbsp. (¼ stick) butter
1 lb. boneless, skinless
   chicken breasts
4 cups snow peas, stringed
   and rinsed
2 carrots, shredded
2 medium onions, chopped

8 oz. sliced mushrooms
¼ cup sour cream
2 tsp. flour
2 Tbsp. soy sauce
hot cooked pasta or rice, for
   serving

Makes:

4 servings

Prep. Time:

15 minutes

Cooking Time:

20-25 minutes

1. In large skillet, melt the butter. Add chicken and fry just until browned on both sides, 8-10 minutes.

2. Remove, cool slightly, and slice into strips.

3. In same skillet, fry onion 3-5 minutes, then add sliced mushrooms and cook 2-3 more minutes.

4. Add chicken, carrots, and peas and cook until desired tenderness, about 10 minutes.

5. In a small bowl, blend together sour cream, flour, and soy sauce.

6. Pour mixture over vegetables in skillet, stir to coat, and cook 2-3 minutes more. Stir frequently.

7. Serve over pasta or rice.

It's "sweatshirt weather"—the season for finishing things. We're butchering the old hens to make way for pullets, filling silo, planting bulbs for next spring's color, picking fall apples, cleaning everything out of the "patch," doing the last hitch of canning.

Old-Fashioned Pot Pie

3-4 lbs. chicken pieces,
   bone-in, skin on
2-3 quarts water
1 tsp. salt
1 large onion, chopped
2 ribs celery, chopped
2 carrots, diced
2 potatoes, diced

¼ cup snipped fresh parsley
salt and pepper, to taste
1 egg
approximately ⅓ cup milk
2 cups all-purpose flour
2 Tbsp. lard or cold butter
2 tsp. baking powder
½ tsp. salt

Makes:

4-6 servings

Prep. Time:

30 minutes

Cooking Time:

50-70 minutes

Note:

I find home-canned chicken and broth convenient for this recipe.

1. In a large saucepan, cover chicken pieces with water. Add 1 tsp. salt. Cook over low heat until chicken is tender, 20-30 minutes. Allow to cool.

2. Remove chicken from bones and cut into bite-sized pieces. Discard skin and bones. Reserve chicken stock.

3. Return chicken to stock.

4. Add onion, celery, carrots, potatoes, and parsley. Season with salt and pepper. Add more water if needed to keep vegetables and chicken covered.

5. Bring to simmer and cook 20-30 minutes, until vegetables are tender.

6. Meanwhile, prepare pot pie squares.

7. Put egg into measuring cup and add enough milk to make ½ cup. Mix.

8. In a good-sized bowl, mix flour, lard or butter, baking powder, and ½ tsp. salt together with pastry blender or fork. Stir in milk and egg. Gather dough into a ball.

9. Roll out dime-thin on lightly floured board. Cut into small squares.

10. Add squares to the hot boiling stew and cook gently until soft, about 10 minutes

BBQ Chicken Pizza

1 pizza crust using recipe on
    page 38
2 Tbsp. olive oil, *divided*
2 boneless, skinless chicken
    breasts, chopped
1 cup chopped green bell peppers
1 cup chopped red bell peppers
1 cup chopped onions
1 cup sliced mushrooms

1 tsp. dried basil
1 tsp. Italian seasoning
    (see recipe on page 270)
1½–2 cups barbecue sauce
    (see recipe on page 129)
1 cup pineapple tidbits,
    drained
3 cups shredded
    mozzarella cheese

Makes:

a 12-inch pizza

Prep. Time:

35 minutes

Baking time:

27 minutes

1. Brown chicken in 1 Tbsp. olive oil in skillet for about 10 minutes, until cooked through. Remove from skillet.

2. Preheat oven to 350°.

3. Stir fry peppers, onions, and mushrooms in 1 Tbsp. olive oil in skillet until crisp-tender, 5–10 minutes.

4. Stir basil and Italian seasoning into vegetables.

5. When crust is parbaked, spread with barbecue sauce.

6. Cover with vegetables and chicken, and layer pineapples over all.

7. Last, top with cheese.

8. Bake in preheated oven for 15 minutes, until cheese is melted and other ingredients are hot.

Easy Summer Veggie Skillet

3 strips bacon, diced
large onion, diced
8 new potatoes, scrubbed and diced
salt to taste
4 cups green *or* yellow beans, snapped in 2" lengths
large zucchini *or* summer squash, diced
2 carrots, shredded
1 lb. diced cooked chicken
1 cup shredded cheddar cheese

Makes:

4-6 servings

Prep. Time:

20 minutes

Cooking Time:

25 minutes

1. In large skillet, fry bacon for 10 minutes.

2. Add onions and potatoes. Sprinkle with salt, cover, and cook about 10 minutes.

3. Add beans and cook 5 more minutes, or until beans are getting tender.

4. Add zucchini, shredded carrots, chicken, and shredded cheese. Stir, cover and cook 5 minutes more, or until hot through.

I like to serve this one-dish meal with a light fruit dessert.

Hash Brown Quiche

3 Tbsp. melted butter

3 cups coarsely shredded raw
  potato

1 cup shredded cheese, Swiss
  or cheddar

¾ cup cooked, diced meat
  such as chicken, ham,
  sausage, *or* bacon

¼ cup diced onion

½ cup milk

½ cup cream

2 eggs

½ tsp. salt

⅛ tsp. pepper

1–2 Tbsp. chopped fresh
  parsley *or* other herb

Makes:

6 servings

Prep. Time:

25 minutes

Baking Time:

45 minutes

Standing Time:

5 minutes

1. Preheat oven to 425°. Grease 9" pie pan.

2. Mix shredded potato and melted butter in pie pan. Press firmly and evenly into the bottom and up the sides of pie pan.

3. Bake in preheated oven for 15 minutes, until potatoes just begin to brown. Remove from oven.

4. Layer into hot crust: cheese, choice of meat, and onion.

5. In a bowl, beat together milk, cream, eggs, salt, and pepper.

6. Pour gently over ingredients in potato crust. Sprinkle with parsley.

7. Return quiche to preheated oven and bake about 30 minutes, or until lightly browned and knife inserted 1 inch from edge comes out clean.

8. Cool 5 minutes before cutting into wedges.

Spinach, Tomato, and Goat Cheese Quiche

unbaked 9" pie shell (see
recipe on page 220)
1 Tbsp. butter
1½ cups chopped fresh
spinach, *divided*
3 eggs
¾ cup heavy cream

¾ cup milk
½ tsp. salt
½ tsp. freshly ground pepper
¾ cup chopped tomato,
divided
1½ cups crumbled feta,
divided

Makes:

6–8 servings

Prep. Time:

15 minutes

Cooking/Baking Time:

55 minutes

Standing Time:

15 minutes

Variation:

Layer half of ⅓ lb.
cooked, crumbled
bacon into quiche
in Steps 4 and 5 for
a BLT flavor.

1. Preheat oven to 350°.

2. In a skillet, melt butter. Sauté spinach lightly.

3. In a bowl, whisk together eggs, cream, milk, salt, and pepper.

4. Layer half the spinach into the pie shell, followed by half the tomatoes, then half the feta.

5. Do a second layer of each item.

6. Pour egg mixture into the pie shell over veggies and cheese.

7. Bake in preheated oven for 40–45 minutes, until a knife stuck in the center comes out clean.

8. Let the quiche stand 15 minutes before serving.

Garden Vegetable Quiche

2½ cups chopped broccoli *or* cauliflower
⅔ cup chopped onions
⅔ cup chopped bell pepper
1¼ cups shredded cheddar cheese
1 cup Bisquick *or* homemade biscuit mix (see recipe on page 33)
3 eggs
2 cups milk
1¼ tsp. salt
½ tsp. pepper

Makes:

6 servings

Prep. Time:

20 minutes

Baking Time:

30–35 minutes

Standing Time:

5–10 minutes

1. Chop broccoli or cauliflower and steam until tender-crisp.

2. Preheat oven to 400°.

3. Combine all vegetables and cheese in a good-sized mixing bowl. Set aside.

4. Combine biscuit mix, eggs, milk, and seasonings. Beat until smooth, about 1 minute.

5. Stir into vegetable mixture.

6. Pour into lightly greased pie pan.

7. Place pan on baking sheet and place in preheated oven for 30–35 minutes, or until golden brown, and a knife inserted near the center comes out clean.

8. Let stand 5–10 minutes before cutting.

Salmon Cakes

8 Tbsp. peanut oil, *divided*
⅓ cup finely chopped onion
2½ cups soft bread crumbs, *divided*
½ cup fresh parsley
½ cup finely chopped red bell pepper
1 pound uncooked salmon fillets
4 oz. smoked salmon, coarsely chopped
1 large egg
1 large egg yolk
1 tsp. Dijon mustard
1 tsp. Worcestershire sauce
1 tsp. hot pepper sauce
¼ tsp. cayenne pepper

Makes:

8-10 servings

Prep. Time:

25 minutes

Chilling Time:

2-4 hours

Cooking Time:

20-40 minutes

1. Heat 4 Tbsp. peanut oil in a 12-inch skillet.

2. Add onion and cook until softened.

3. Transfer to a large bowl.

4. Mix in 1¼ cups bread crumbs, parsley, and red bell pepper.

5. Gently mix in both types of salmon. Carefully stir in egg, yolk, mustard, Worcestershire, hot pepper sauce, and cayenne pepper.

6. Cover and refrigerate until well chilled, 2-4 hours. Divide mixture into 10 cakes, flattening each into a circle.

7. Coat cakes in remaining bread crumbs.

8. Heat 2 Tbsp. peanut oil in cleaned skillet over medium heat.

9. Cook a few fish cakes at a time until golden brown on both sides and cooked through. Serve cakes with tartar sauce (see recipe to the right).

Tartar Sauce

¾ cup mayonnaise (see recipe on page 65)
2 Tbsp. sweet pickle relish
1–2 Tbsp. chopped fresh tarragon
1 tsp. fresh lemon juice
grated zest of 1 lemon
¼ tsp. hot pepper sauce

1. Mix all ingredients in a small bowl.

2. Cover and refrigerate for at least 1 hour to allow flavors to blend.

Makes:

a scant cup

Prep. Time:

10 minutes

Chilling Time:

1 hour or more

I also serve this with fried fish from our pond. I just flour the fillets liberally and fry them in butter. Salt and pepper generously.

Sauce for Burgers

1 cup ketchup
1½ tsp. Worcestershire sauce
½ cup brown sugar
¼ cup honey
¼ tsp. liquid smoke
2 tsp. prepared mustard
¼ tsp. salt
⅛ tsp. pepper

Makes:

1½ cups

Prep. Time:

10 minutes

Blend all ingredients together. Apply liberally to burgers while grilling.

Meat Marinade

1½ cups teriyaki sauce
¾ cup soy sauce
½ cup lemon juice
½ cup apple cider vinegar
¼ cup Worcestershire sauce

2 Tbsp. dry mustard
2½ tsp. salt
1 Tbsp. pepper
1½ Tbsp. parsley flakes
2 cloves garlic, minced

Makes:

3 cups

Prep. Time:

10 minutes

1. Mix all ingredients.

2. Marinate meat in mixture 6 to 8 hours before grilling. Great for chicken breasts, steaks, and pork chops.

Barbecue Sauce

2 cups ketchup
1 cup brown sugar
¼ cup chopped onion

½ tsp. garlic powder
½ tsp. liquid smoke

Makes:

2½ cups

Combine all ingredients and stir until sugar dissolves. This sauce needs to be cooked along with whatever dish you are making, so use it in casseroles or brushed on meat during grilling. We especially like it on burgers.

Chicken Marinade for Barbecued Chicken

3 cups water
¾ cup vinegar
¼ cup sugar
¾ cup (1½ sticks) butter
1 Tbsp. Worcestershire sauce
1 Tbsp. garlic salt
¼ cup salt
1 Tbsp. black pepper

1. Mix all ingredients together in a saucepan.

2. Cook until sugar is dissolved and butter is melted.

3. Pour over chicken. Marinate bone-in chicken 24 hours in the refrigerator and boneless skinless chicken for 12 hours. Grill.

Makes:

enough for 10 lbs. of chicken

Prep. Time:

15 minutes

Cooking Time:

10–15 minutes

Marinating Time:

12–24 hours

The "FARM HOME" Cookbook

VEGETABLES

Fresh vegetables gathered in your own garden or at the farmer's market are delicious and so good for you. If you are on a low-salt diet, you can easily eat fresh vegetables plain. Children growing up with vegetables cannot help but love them. Get your children involved in your garden or shopping at the farmers' market. When they're acquainted with vegetables early on—including their sources when possible—they'll come to enjoy them and expect them.

The secret to cooking delicious vegetables and preserving all their nutrients is to use small amounts of water and low cooking temperatures. Discarding the excess water that the vegetables cooked in is discarding nutrients. It's easier to cook with minimal water, providing the skillet or saucepan is not too large in proportion to the amount of vegetables. So choose the size pan or skillet based on the amount of vegetables you're cooking. For example—3 cups carrots in a 1-quart saucepan.

Wash all vegetables, and let them stand in cold water until you're ready to cook them. Drain them just before putting them in the pot.

CARROTS Bring ½" water to a boil. Add 4 cups freshly drained, sliced carrots and return to a boil. Turn heat to low and simmer, covered, for approximately 10 minutes. Add a dab of butter just before serving if desired.

BEETS Scrub beets well. Don't peel them, but trim off all but 1" of the stem. Leave the taproot on. Place 1" of water in skillet with beets, and bring to a boil. Reduce heat. Simmer covered until beets are tender. Medium or small beets take 25-30 minutes. Cool, trim stem, and peel (easily done with your hands). Then cut in small chunks. Add seasonings and browned butter if desired, and reheat.

PEAS After you've shelled the peas, wash in cold water. Drain, then put in skillet with a small amount of water (½ cup to 4 cups peas). Bring to boil, cover, reduce heat to simmer, and steam for 10 minutes. Season and add butter if desired. Do *not* drain.

GREEN BEANS Put washed and drained fresh green beans in a skillet; add ½ cup water to 5-6 cups beans. Bring to boiling, turn to low, and simmer for 10 minutes until tender-crisp. Add desired seasonings and a pat of butter.

SWEET CORN The highlight of summer! Cut corn off the cob with a sharp knife, scraping the cob to get all the goodness. Melt 2 Tbsp. butter in a saucepan, add 5 cups of corn, 1 tsp. salt, and ½ cup water. Bring to a boil, reduce heat to low, simmer for 10 minutes. For special tastiness, stir in 2 oz. of cream cheese.

CORN-ON-THE-COB Put an inch of water in the bottom of a large kettle (kettle size according to how many ears you are preparing) and set the ears in upright if your kettle is tall enough—one ear with the point down, the next pointed up, and so on. You can get more in a kettle that way. But if you do not have a deep kettle put the ears in criss-cross—one layer one way, the next the other way. The idea is to steam the corn, and make sure the steam can reach each ear. Put the lid on your kettle and steam for 15 minutes. (If you have several dozen ears, then steam for 5-10 minutes longer.) The ears will be very hot, so put the corn on plates to cool a bit, then butter liberally and salt each ear as you go. Serve with glasses of cold milk, and your meal is complete.

CAULIFLOWER AND BROCCOLI
These two vegetables need only several tablespoons of water added to the florets. Always cover your saucepan so no steam escapes. Bring to a boil, then simmer for 5 minutes. These are also wonderful in stir fries and eaten raw.

NEW POTATOES Red potatoes cooked in their skins are especially good when they're the size of golf balls. Cook them like other vegetables with a small amount of water in a covered pan. Bring to a boil, then reduce heat, and simmer for 15-20 minutes. My husband likes to flatten them with a fork, add butter, salt, and pepper, then pour fresh cold Jersey milk over all.

Creamed Peas

4 cups fresh peas
½ cup water
2 Tbsp. (¼ stick) butter
1½ tsp. all-purpose flour

2 tsp. sugar
1 tsp. salt
¼ tsp. pepper
milk or cream

Makes:

4–6 servings

Cooking Time:

10–15 minutes

1. Cook peas 5 minutes in water. Drain, saving cooking water.

2. In another saucepan, melt butter. Blend in flour and seasonings.

3. Add enough cream or milk to reserved cooking water to make one cup.

4. Stir into mixture. Bring to a boil, stirring constantly.

5. Add white sauce to peas. Heat through.

New Peas and Tiny Potatoes

4 strips bacon
1¼ cups shelled new peas
1¼ lbs. tiny new potatoes
2 young carrots, diced
½ cup milk
¼ cup heavy cream
3 tsp. cornstarch
salt and pepper, to taste

Makes:

4 servings

Prep. Time:

10 minutes

Cooking Time:

25 minutes

1. Fry bacon until crisp. Drain on paper towels.

2. Boil potatoes in their jackets in salted water until fork-tender. Drain and keep warm.

3. Place carrots with ¼ cup water in saucepan, then top with peas and lightly salt.

4. Cover and steam about 3-4 minutes. Do not drain.

5. Mix milk, cream, and cornstarch together until smooth. Then stir into peas and carrots.

6. Heat just until thickened.

7. Pour over hot potatoes. Salt and pepper to taste, then top with bacon bits.

Note:

The young carrots are mainly for color. If you don't have any, you can skip them.

Summer Squash with Garlic and Basil

2 Tbsp. olive oil
4 garlic cloves, minced
4 small summer squash, very thinly sliced
4 Tbsp. chopped fresh basil

1. Heat olive oil in medium frying pan over medium heat. Add garlic.

2. Add and sauté summer squash quickly.

3. Stir basil in quickly and serve immediately.

Makes:

2–3 servings

Prep. Time:

5 minutes

Cooking Time:

5 minutes

Tip: *How to Sauté*

Sautéing releases flavor from aromatic vegetables like onions, leeks, garlic, and mushrooms, which will later flavor a dish. Sautéing is quick and healthy. It uses just a little fat—usually 1 tablespoon—and the entire sautéed preparation is added to the dish, so any vitamins that leach out while cooking the vegetables get into the meal in the end.

To sauté, heat oil or butter over medium heat in a heavy-bottomed pan. Drop the vegetable in; if the temperature is right, it should sizzle. (Sauté is a French word that means jump.) If it smokes, the pan is too hot. If the temperature is right, add the remaining vegetables and turn the heat down to medium-low. (On an electric stove, set another burner to medium low and transfer the entire pan to that burner at this point.) Stir often until the vegetables have softened to your liking—this should take 5-10 minutes.

Zucchini Fritters

1 cup shredded zucchini
2 Tbsp. minced onions
1 carrot, shredded
1 egg
½ cup all-purpose flour
¼ tsp. seasoning salt
⅛ tsp. garlic salt
salt and pepper, to taste
butter, for frying

1. Stir everything together in a bowl except butter.

2. Add butter to skillet and melt.

3. Drop vegetable mixture by tablespoonsful into hot buttered skillet.

4. Fry on both sides until nicely browned.

Makes:

2 servings

Prep. Time:

10 minutes

Cooking Time:

10–15 minutes

Variation:

Add cooked meat of your choice to Step 1 for a good dish, too.

Lemon Garlic Brussels Sprouts

3 Tbsp. butter
1 lb. Brussel sprouts, halved
1 small onion, chopped
1-2 garlic cloves

3 Tbsp. lemon juice
salt and pepper, to taste
Parmesan cheese, for
   sprinkling

Makes:

4 servings

Cooking Time:

12-14 minutes

1. Melt butter in skillet. Sauté sprouts and onion in butter for 5 minutes.

2. Add garlic, lemon juice, salt, and pepper. Sauté for another minute.

3. Reduce heat and cook for 5-6 minutes until tender.

4. Sprinkle with cheese. Serve.

Broccoli with Buttered Crumbs

2 Tbsp. (¼ stick) butter
1 cup fresh bread crumbs
¼ cup chopped fresh parsley
1 tsp. minced fresh rosemary *or* ½ tsp. dried
salt and pepper, to taste
1½ lbs. broccoli, cut into florets
2 tsp. melted butter
1 Tbsp. lemon juice

Makes:

4-6 servings

Prep. Time:

10 minutes

Cooking Time:

15 minutes

1. Melt 2 Tbsp. butter in heavy skillet over low heat.

2. Add the bread crumbs and cook, stirring constantly, until they are golden brown.

3. Transfer to a bowl.

4. Blend parsley and rosemary, then combine with crumbs. Season with salt and pepper.

5. Separately, steam the broccoli with ¼ cup water for 5 minutes, or just until tender-crisp.

6. Remove to a warm serving dish. Stir in the melted butter and lemon juice. If needed add salt and pepper to taste.

7. Top with breadcrumb mixture and serve.

Creamy Cabbage

6 cups shredded cabbage
¼ cup chopped onion
⅓ cup water
½ tsp. salt
3 ounces cream cheese, cubed
2 Tbsp. (¼ stick) butter
½ tsp. celery seed
paprika

Makes:

4 servings

Prep. Time:

10 minutes

Cooking Time:

7 minutes

1. Combine cabbage, onion, water, and salt in saucepan. Cook 7 minutes until crisp-tender.

2. Add cream cheese, butter, celery seeds, and paprika. Toss lightly until cream cheese and butter are mostly melted. Serve.

This fall I had a row of Chinese cabbage in the garden. I cut the oblong heads from the roots last week and put them in our farm shop where it's cool but not freezing. We think Chinese cabbage is a much under-rated vegetable.

Cheesy Chard

1 lb. Swiss chard *or* spinach, torn or cut into pieces
4 eggs, beaten
1 cup milk
1 cup shredded Swiss cheese
¼ cup grated Parmesan cheese
1 cup small bread cubes
½ cup sliced green onions

Makes:

4 servings

Prep. Time:

20 minutes

Cooking/Baking Time:

35–40 minutes

1. Preheat oven to 375°.

2. In a saucepan, steam Swiss chard in a small amount of water until just tender. Drain. Set aside.

3. Combine rest of ingredients in mixing bowl. Stir in steamed vegetable.

4. Pour into greased 9" × 9" baking dish. Cover and bake in preheated oven until set, 25–30 minutes.

5. Uncover and bake 5 minutes more to allow top to brown.

Glazed Carrots

3 cups carrots, cut in strips
2 Tbsp. (¼ stick) butter

¼ cup brown sugar
salt and pepper, to taste

Makes:

4 servings

Prep. Time:

5 minutes

Cooking Time:

13 minutes

1. Cook carrot strips in saucepan with ½ cup water for 8 minutes or until crisp-tender. Drain.

2. Blend butter and sugar in a heavy skillet over low heat. Add carrots.

3. Cook over low heat 5 minutes, turning carrots to coat all sides with syrup.

4. Sprinkle with salt and pepper to taste.

Broccoli Florets with Cherry Tomatoes

1½ lbs. broccoli
1-2 Tbsp. butter
12 cherry tomatoes
2 fresh basil leaves, chopped,
    or ¼ tsp. dried

salt and freshly ground
    pepper, to taste
juice of ½ lemon

Makes:

4 servings

Prep. Time:

10 minutes

Cooking Time:

10 minutes

1. Cut broccoli into bite-size florets.

2. Steam in ¼ cup water until tender-crisp. Rinse in cold water to maintain color.

3. Drain. Just before serving, melt butter in skillet. Then add florets, cherry tomatoes, and basil.

4. Toss until heated through. Sprinkle with lemon juice, salt, and pepper. Toss again and serve immediately.

Veggie Stir Fry

4 tsp. cornstarch
1 cup cold water
½ cup soy sauce
2 Tbsp. (¼ stick) butter
2 medium carrots, sliced
1 small onion, chopped

2 cups shredded cabbage
8 mushrooms, sliced
2 cups broccoli florets
1 tsp. minced garlic
hot cooked rice, for serving

Makes:

4 servings

Prep. Time:

10 minutes

Cooking Time:

10-15 minutes

1. In a small bowl, whisk cornstarch, water, and soy sauce together until smooth.

2. Add butter to a large skillet. Stir fry carrots, onion, cabbage, and mushrooms for 5 minutes.

3. Add broccoli and garlic. Stir fry until vegetables are crispy tender.

4. Stir soy sauce mixture together again. Add to skillet. Cook and stir until thickened.

5. Serve over rice.

Corn Fritters

½ cup all-purpose flour
½ tsp. baking powder
1 pinch salt
¼ cup milk
1 egg
2 Tbsp. maple syrup, plus more for serving
2 cups fresh corn kernels
3 Tbsp. butter

Makes:

2-4 servings

Prep. Time:

15 minutes

Cooking Time:

10-15 minutes

1. In large bowl sift flour, baking powder, and salt together. Add milk and whisk until smooth.

2. Beat in egg and maple syrup. Gently mix in corn.

3. Melt butter in large skillet. Make fritters by dropping 2-3 tablespoons batter for each fritter into hot butter. Cook on each side until golden brown.

4. Serve hot with maple syrup.

Don't we all look forward to sweet corn? Hal Borland says it well in *Sundial of the Seasons*: "Hurry it to the pot, watch it like a hawk, dash it to the table. Then eat. And ceremony is forgotten. So is conversation, for the first few ears, at least. After that you catch your breath and thank the Indians. Then you start all over again."

Corn, Bacon, and Sour Cream Bake

3 cups fresh corn kernels
2 Tbsp. (¼ stick) butter
2 Tbsp. chopped onion
2 Tbsp. all-purpose flour
8 oz. sour cream
½ tsp. salt
6 slices thick bacon, cooked, drained, and crumbled, *divided*

1. Cook corn in a little water for 4 minutes. Drain and set aside.

2. Preheat oven to 350°.

3. Melt butter in large saucepan. Add onion and sauté until soft. Add flour and cook, stirring for 1 minute.

4. Add corn, sour cream, salt and half the bacon, stirring until combined.

5. Pour into greased 2-quart baking dish. Top with remaining bacon.

6. Bake in preheated oven for 30 minutes or until top is slightly browned.

Makes:

4 servings

Prep. Time:

5-10 minutes

Cooking Time:

10 minutes

Baking Time:

30 minutes

Variation:

Use canned or frozen corn instead of fresh.

German Sweet-Sour Beans

1 lb. fresh *or* frozen green beans, *or* 1 quart canned green beans
2 strips bacon
1 cup minced onion
1 Tbsp. all-purpose flour
½ cup bean liquid
¼ cup water
¼ cup apple cider vinegar
2 Tbsp. sugar
1 tsp. salt
¼ tsp. pepper

Makes:

4 servings

Prep. Time:

10 minutes

Cooking Time:

15 minutes

1. If using fresh or frozen beans, cook 15 minutes until tender. Reserve cooking water.

2. In large pan or skillet, brown bacon until crisp. Remove bacon, crumble, and set aside. Keep drippings in pan.

3. Sauté onion in bacon drippings until golden.

4. Stir in flour. Add reserved bean cooking liquid, water, vinegar, and seasonings. Bring to boil, stirring til slightly thickened.

5. Stir in beans. Heat through.

6. Sprinkle with crisp bacon bits just before serving.

Green Beans with Warm Mustard Vinaigrette

1 lb. fresh green beans with ends trimmed
1 shallot, minced
1 Tbsp. Dijon mustard
1 Tbsp. balsamic vinegar
¼ cup olive oil
½ tsp. salt
freshly ground pepper
2 Tbsp. fresh snipped dill

Makes:
_____

4-6 servings

Prep. Time:
_____

10 minutes

Cooking Time:
_____

10 minutes

1. Bring a large pot of lightly salted water to a boil. Add green beans.

2. Cook until just crisp, 3 to 5 minutes. Drain well.

3. While beans are cooking, combine mustard, vinegar, olive oil, salt, and pepper in a small saucepan over medium heat.

4. Stir constantly until mixture is hot and begins to steam.

5. Toss hot dressing with drained green beans. Add dill. Serve immediately.

I'm doing something different this year. I'm collecting seeds. I'm going to plant a "scatter garden" in the next month or so.

Oven Baked Beans

2 cups dried navy beans
8 cups cold water
1 tsp. salt, *divided*
½ lb. salt pork *or* bacon
½ cup finely chopped onions
½ cup finely chopped green bell pepper
½ cup finely chopped celery
⅔ cup brown sugar
1 tsp. dry mustard
½ cup dark molasses
¼ tsp. pepper

Makes:

4–6 servings

Prep. Time:

15 minutes

Soaking Time:

overnight

Cooking/Baking Time:

3½ hours

1. Rinse beans. Soak in water overnight.

2. The next morning, add ½ tsp. salt to beans and soaking water. Bring to boil in saucepan.

3. Reduce heat and simmer, covered, 1 hour. Drain, reserving cooking liquid.

4. Preheat oven to 300°

5. Mix rest of ingredients in large bowl, including remaining ½ tsp. salt and 2 cups cooking liquid. (Reserve any cooking liquid that remains.)

6. Pour into greased 2½-quart baking dish. Cover and bake in preheated oven 2½ hours, stirring occasionally, or until beans are as thick as desired.

7. Add more cooking liquid from Step 3 if too dry.

Cucumber Salad and New Potatoes

2-3 lbs. new potatoes
1 cup salad dressing (see recipe on page 64)
½ cup honey
¼ cup apple cider vinegar
½ cup milk
2-3 cucumbers, peeled and sliced
butter
salt and pepper

Makes:

4-6 servings

Prep. Time:

10 minutes

1. Boil new potatoes until soft. While these are cooking, prepare salad.

2. Mix salad dressing, honey, vinegar, and milk to make a creamy, fairly thick dressing. Add a little more milk if needed.

3. Pour dressing over cucumbers. Mix gently together.

4. To serve, each person mashes cooked potatoes on plate with fork, seasons with salt, pepper, and butter, and spoons cucumber salad on top.

This is a family favorite!

In my early garden I plant just enough for fresh eating: two kinds of peas, onions, radishes, parsley, three or four kinds of lettuce, red potatoes, spinach, carrots, cabbage, broccoli, and beets. And later beans, one summer squash plant, an early tomato plant, cucumber plants, plus basil and other herbs.

Baked Potato Spears with Dip

2 medium potatoes, peeled
　　or not
6 Tbsp. salad dressing
　　(see recipe on page 64)
onion salt
pepper

Dip:
¾ cup salad dressing
6 Tbsp. finely grated
　　Parmesan cheese
6 Tbsp. milk
2 tsp. snipped chives

Makes:

2 servings

Prep. Time:

5 minutes

Baking Time:

50 minutes

1. Preheat oven to 375°.

2. Cut potatoes lengthwise into wedges. Brush with salad dressing and season with onion salt and pepper.

3. Place on greased baking sheet and bake in preheated oven for 50 minutes.

4. Serve with dip.

A local man told us to always lay seed potatoes out on a table for several weeks before planting. Then the eyes will sprout green shoots, making it so much easier to know where to make the cuts before planting.

Parmesan Potato Wedges

8 medium potatoes
olive oil
1 cup grated Parmesan
    cheese

1 Tbsp. paprika
½ tsp. pepper
1½ tsp. salt
1 tsp. garlic salt

1. Preheat oven to 350°.

2. Wash and cut unpeeled potatoes into wedges.

3. Brush a large baking sheet with olive oil.

4. Place potato wedges on baking sheet in one layer. Brush with olive oil.

5. Mix together Parmesan and seasonings and sprinkle over potatoes.

6. Bake in preheated oven for 1½ hours or until potatoes are tender.

Makes:

8 servings

Prep. Time:

10 minutes

Baking Time:

1½ hours

Variation:

Serve with a dip of your choice. These are also good garnished with bacon crumbles and shredded cheese.

Golden Brown Chive Roasted Potatoes

6 large potatoes
¼ cup (half stick) butter, melted
½ tsp. salt
1 Tbsp. freshly chopped chives
½ cup shredded cheese
3 Tbsp. bread crumbs

Makes:

6 servings

Prep. Time:

20 minutes

Baking Time:

1½ hours

Variation:

You may peel the potatoes ahead of time and hold them in a bowl of cold water until ready to use. Dry thoroughly.

1. Preheat oven to 350°. Cover a baking sheet with foil. Grease foil. Peel potatoes. Cut a thin slice off the long side of each potato so it can sit flat.

2. With a sharp knife cut vertical slits from the top almost through to the bottom of each potato, being careful not to cut through the whole way. Make slits ¼–½" apart.

3. Dip cut potatoes in melted butter. Place on foil-covered baking sheet. Sprinkle each potato with salt.

4. Bake in preheated oven for 1 hour and 15 minutes, basting with remaining butter. The potatoes will turn a crisp golden brown, and the slits will open in accordion fashion as they bake.

5. Combine chives, cheese, and bread crumbs and stuff them into the slits in the potatoes to form a delicious topping.

6. Bake 15 minutes longer.

7. Serve immediately and expect the diners to ignore everything else on their plates.

Santa Fe Roasted Potatoes

2½ lbs. red-skinned potatoes,
 unpeeled, cut in 1" cubes
1 Tbsp. finely chopped garlic
1 tsp. dried oregano
1 tsp. chili powder
½ tsp. cumin

¼ tsp. pepper
½ tsp. salt
2 dashes cayenne pepper,
 optional
¼ cup olive oil

Makes:

6 servings

Prep. Time:

10 minutes

Baking Time:

1 hour

1. Preheat oven to 350°.

2. Place potatoes in greased 9" × 13" baking pan.

3. Combine remaining ingredients in a bowl.

4. Pour over potatoes. Toss to coat.

5. Bake uncovered in preheated oven for 1 hour, stirring every 15 minutes.

Campfire Potatoes

6 medium potatoes, peeled or not, thinly sliced
1 medium onion, diced
6 Tbsp. (¾ stick) butter
½ cup shredded cheese of your choice
2 Tbsp. snipped fresh parsley
1 tsp. Worcestershire sauce
salt and pepper, to taste
½ cup chicken broth

Makes:

6-8 servings

Prep. Time:

20 minutes

Grilling Time:

35-40 minutes

1. Place potatoes and onion on a large piece of heavy-duty foil (about 20" × 20"). Dot with butter.

2. Combine cheese, parsley, Worcestershire sauce, salt, and pepper in a bowl. Sprinkle over potatoes.

3. Fold foil up around potatoes and add broth. Seal edges of foil well.

4. Grill packet over medium coals for 35–40 minutes or until potatoes are tender.

Skillet Scalloped Potatoes

3 Tbsp. butter
6 potatoes, peeled or not, thinly sliced
1 tsp. salt, *or more to taste*
¼ tsp. pepper

2 cups milk
1 cup shredded cheese of your choice

Makes:

6–8 servings

Prep. Time:

10 minutes

Cooking Time:

20–30 minutes

1. Fry potatoes in butter in large skillet until almost tender and slightly browned, stirring often.

2. Sprinkle with salt and pepper.

3. Pour milk over all. Boil gently until milk is absorbed.

4. Sprinkle with cheese.

Creamy Potato Gratin

8 cloves garlic
2½ cups heavy whipping cream
1 cup milk
pinch nutmeg
3½ lbs. baking potatoes, about 8 large potatoes
salt and pepper
½ cup grated Parmesan cheese

Makes:

8 servings

Prep. Time:

20 minutes

Standing Time:

40 minutes

Cooking/Baking Time:

1 hour, 45 minutes

1. Put garlic cloves in saucepan, cover with water, and bring to a boil. Pour water out, leaving garlic in pan.

2. Add cream, milk, and nutmeg to garlic. Cook over low heat until cream begins to simmer.

3. Turn off heat. Let cream mixture stand at room temperature until flavors are blended, about 30 minutes.

4. Discard garlic.

5. Preheat oven to 350°.

6. Meanwhile, peel potatoes and cut into ⅛"-thick slices. Sprinkle with salt and pepper.

7. Arrange a layer of potatoes in generously buttered 9" × 13" baking dish, overlapping the slices.

8. Pour ⅔ cup cream mixture over potatoes. Make several more layers of potatoes and cream, using all of both.

9. Sprinkle cheese over top.

10. Cover baking dish tightly with lid or aluminum foil. Bake in preheated oven 45 minutes.

11. Uncover. Continue baking until potatoes are browned and tender, 45 to 55 minutes more.

12. Let gratin rest 10 minutes before serving.

Honey Glazed Sweet Potatoes

2 lbs. sweet potatoes, cut into ½" cubes
6 Tbsp. (¾ stick) butter, melted
1 tsp. fresh lemon juice
3 Tbsp. honey
salt and pepper, to taste

Makes:

4-6 servings

Prep. Time:

10 minutes

Baking Time:

20-30 minutes

1. Preheat oven to 425°.

2. Mix all ingredients together. Put in a greased 2- or 3-quart baking dish.

3. Bake, covered, in preheated oven 20-30 minutes, or until potatoes are tender.

Brown Rice with Mint and Chives

1 cup uncooked brown rice
2 cups water
½ tsp. salt
1 cup slivered almonds
2 Tbsp. fresh snipped chives
2 Tbsp. finely chopped fresh mint
¼ cup olive oil

1. Combine rice, water, and salt in saucepan.

2. Bring to a boil. Turn heat to low, cover, and simmer 45 minutes. It's better not to peek.

3. Turn off burner and allow to sit, covered, for 15 minutes. Fluff with fork.

4. Add rest of ingredients. Stir gently.

Makes:

2–4 servings

Prep. Time:

5 minutes

Cooking Time:

1 hour

Note:

Deliciously different!

Yesterday was Ascension Day, and we had a family gathering. As I glanced over the array of food, I realized how much of it came from our gardens. The fresh lettuce and onions that garnished the burgers (plus cheese from a local cheesemaker); baked beans—made with assorted beans, tomatoes, onions, peppers, all from last year's garden; potato salad, with potatoes from last year's crop; fresh rhubarb for a dandy dessert; fresh mint tea; and, of course, lots of shade-grown coffee (raised by some, albeit distant, small farmer).

The "Farm Home" Cookbook

CANNED and PICKLED DELIGHTS

Hot Pepper Rings

Hungarian Yellow Wax peppers *or* jalapenos, sliced into rings, enough to fill 6 pint jars

6 tsp. non-iodized salt, *divided*

6 tsp. olive oil, *divided*

2 cups white vinegar

3 cups water

3 cups sugar

1. Wearing kitchen gloves, slice peppers into rings and discard seeds.

2. Fill 6 pint jars.

3. Put 1 tsp. salt and 1 tsp. olive oil in each jar.

4. In a saucepan, mix together vinegar, water, and sugar and bring to boil. Stir to make sure sugar is dissolved.

5. Pour boiling brine into jars.

6. Process in water bath according to your canner's instructions.

Makes:

6 pints

Prep. Time:

25 minutes

Cooking Time:

20 minutes

Processing Time:

see your canner's manual

One year when the children were still all at home, our apple trees were abundantly fruitful. We canned 200 quarts of applesauce, plus apple butter and pie filling. A friend brought us his little cider press, and Michael, who was 12 at the time, made sure we had fresh cider every day.

Lemon Dill Beans

1 lb. fresh green string beans
1 lb. fresh yellow string beans
2½ cups apple cider vinegar
1¼ cups water
1 Tbsp. non-iodized salt
1 Tbsp. sugar
3-4 tsp. pickling spice, *divided*
3-4 large strips lemon zest, *divided*
3-4 heads fresh dill, *divided*

Makes:

3-4 pints

Prep. Time:

20 minutes

Cooking Time:

15 minutes

Processing Time:

See your canner's manual

1. Trim the beans into 4" lengths to fit into pint canning jars.

2. Combine vinegar, water, salt, and sugar in large saucepan and bring to a boil over high heat.

3. Meanwhile, add 1 tsp. pickling spice, 1 strip lemon zest, and 1 dill head to each pint jar.

4. Tightly pack trimmed beans into jars.

5. Pour boiling pickling liquid into jars and process according to your canner's directions.

Sweet Pickle Spears

4 lbs. 3-4"-long cucumbers, cut length-wise into spears
2 Tbsp. non-iodized salt
4 tsp. celery seed
4 tsp. turmeric
4 cups sugar
1½ tsp. mustard seed
3¾ cups apple cider vinegar

Makes:

6-8 pints

Prep. Time:

30 minutes

Standing Time:

2 hours

Cooking Time:

20 minutes

Processing Time:

See your canner's manual

1. Cover cucumbers with boiling water in large bowl. Let stand 2 hours. Drain.

2. Combine remaining ingredients in a large saucepan. Bring to a boil.

3. Pack cucumbers into hot jars, leaving ¼" headspace.

4. Ladle hot liquid over cucumbers. Remove air bubbles by slipping a table knife down between pickle spears and side of jar. Do this in a complete circle inside the jar.

5. Process according to your canner's directions.

We are more apt to have pickles on the table for lunch or supper when we have sandwiches or soups. If not on sandwiches, we eat them with a fork. Cheese and pickles go together like bread and butter!

Dill Pickles

4 lbs. 4"-long cucumbers
6 Tbsp. non-iodized salt
4½ cups water
4 cups apple cider vinegar

14 heads fresh dill
3½ tsp. mustard seed
14 peppercorns

Makes:

7 pints

Prep. Time:

25 minutes

Cooking Time:

25 minutes

Processing Time:

See your canner's manual

1. Cut cucumbers into ¼" thick spears or coins.

2. Combine salt, water, and vinegar in a large pot. Bring to boil.

3. Pack cucumbers into hot jars, leaving ¼" headspace.

4. To each jar add 2 heads of dill, ½ tsp. mustard seed, and 2 peppercorns. (These can be put in bottom of jar instead if you prefer.)

5. Ladle hot liquid over cucumbers. Remove air bubbles by running a table knife in a circle inside the jar between the pickles and jar side.

6. Process according to your canner's directions.

We can a lot of pickles especially for the noon meal that follows our church services. Here's our menu for our church meal: homemade bread, butter, jam or peanut butter spread, pickles, pickled beets, cheese (usually two varieties), and cold meat of some kind. Then we also have coffee and sometimes garden (mint) tea, too. The meal is topped off with pies made by the church women. It's a meal we always enjoy even though we don't often have it at home.

Hamburger Pickles

1 cup non-iodized salt
1 gallon hot water
1 gallon cucumbers, thinly sliced
2 Tbsp. alum
2½ cups apple cider vinegar
2½ cups water
3 cups sugar
1 Tbsp. celery seed
1 stick cinnamon
1 Tbsp. whole cloves
1 Tbsp. mixed pickling spice

Makes:

4 quarts or 8 pints

Prep. Time:

A drawn-out affair, but the pickles are delicious!

Processing Time:

See your canner's manual

1. Make salt brine by combining salt and hot water. When salt is dissolved and brine has cooled down, add sliced cucumbers. Set aside, covered, at room temperature.

2. After 3-5 days, drain. Wash cucumber slices in cold water 4 times. Be sure to get all the salt off.

3. Place drained cucumber slices in stockpot with alum and water to cover.

4. Cover. Boil 10 minutes.

5. Drain. Rinse cucumber slices in warm water.

6. Make syrup in stockpot by combining vinegar, 2½ cups water, and sugar. Place spices in spice bag and drop into syrup.

7. Heat syrup to boiling. Add cucumber slices. Boil until clear, about 20 minutes.

8. Place cucumber slices and syrup in jars. Process according to your canner's directions.

Refrigerator Pickles

7 cups unpeeled, thinly sliced cucumbers

1 cup thinly sliced onions

1 cup diced green bell peppers

1 cup apple cider vinegar

1½ cups sugar

1 Tbsp. celery seed

2 tsp. non-iodized salt

Makes:

10 cups

Prep. Time:

30 minutes

1. Put vegetables in 2 large jars or containers with lids.

2. Mix together vinegar and sugar in mixing bowl. Do not heat. When sugar is dissolved, add celery seed and salt. Stir until salt dissolves.

3. Pour brine over vegetables.

4. Refrigerate, covered, at least 24 hours before eating. These keep in the refrigerator for months if you're careful to always use a clean utensil to fish them out.

Our girls came home one day recently, and we made sauerkraut. Gallons and gallons of it. When the fermentation is completed, we'll divide the kraut among the families. We'll can some, and the rest we'll eat right out of the crocks!

Chili Sauce

24 medium tomatoes
7 medium onions
4 sweet bell peppers; 2 green and 2 red look nice
2 cups sugar
4 cups apple cider vinegar
2 Tbsp. non-iodized salt
pepper, and other fresh *or* dried herbs to taste

1. Drop tomatoes in boiling water. Remove after one minute. Their skins will peel off easily.

2. Chop vegetables very finely by hand or in a salsa maker. Place in large stockpot.

3. Add rest of ingredients to stockpot. Simmer uncovered together for several hours to blend flavors and thicken.

4. Stir occasionally.

5. Can in pints—following directions in your canning manual.

I use chili sauce when I make chili soup, sloppy joes, spaghetti, baked beans, etc. It's good on eggs and yum-a setti, too. Sometimes I use it instead of ketchup.

Makes:

10–12 pints

Prep. Time:

30 minutes

Cooking Time:

2 hours

Processing Time:

See your canner's manual

Variation:

I use this same recipe for salsa but add some hot peppers. Whether making chili sauce or salsa, I also like to add parsley, oregano, and thyme, or whatever herbs I have on hand. Taste it until it is just right for you. I just love to play with herbs!

Cucumber Relish

6 large cucumbers
4 large onions
4 large sweet bell peppers
2 Tbsp. salt
1 Tbsp. celery seed
2 cups apple cider vinegar
2 cups sugar
½ tsp. turmeric
2 Tbsp. non-iodized salt
1 Tbsp. dry mustard

1. Grind cucumbers, onions, and peppers. I use a hand-cranked meat grinder outside at the picnic table, but a food processor works, too. Just process the vegetables into tiny chopped pieces, but not mush.

2. Add salt and let stand overnight at room temperature.

3. The next morning place mixture in strainer to drain. Rinse with water, and then drain again.

4. Place vegetable mixture in saucepan. Add remaining ingredients.

5. Cover and bring to a simmer.

6. Uncover and cook over low heat 30-40 minutes, stirring occasionally, until nicely thickened.

7. Place hot mixture in sterilized jars. Then process according to your canner's instructions.

Makes:

6 half-pints

Prep. Time:

30 minutes

Standing Time:

overnight

Cooking Time:

40-50 minutes

Processing Time:

See your canner's manual

Mrs. Hoover's Sweet Cauliflower Mix

1 head cauliflower, divided in small florets
I lb. carrots, sliced in coins *or* short sticks
5-quart ice cream pail of sliced cucumbers
3 cups water
1 cup white vinegar
3 cups sugar
2 Tbsp. non-iodized salt
½ tsp. turmeric

1. Steam cauliflower briefly in small amount of water just until crisp-tender. Set aside to cool.

2. Do the same with carrots. (Do not cook the cucumbers!)

3. Mix vegetables together.

4. Pack in jars, allowing 1" of headspace.

5. In a saucepan, mix together water, vinegar, sugar, salt, and turmeric. Bring to a boil. Make sure sugar and salt have dissolved.

6. Fill jars and process according to your canner's directions.

Makes:

8 quarts

Prep. Time:

30 minutes

Cooking Time:

30 minutes

Processing Time:

See your canner's manual

Variation:

Dill seed (½ tsp.) and a garlic clove can be added per quart.

Pepper Butter

3½ lbs. Hungarian Yellow Wax peppers, 40–45 peppers
4 cups white vinegar
4 cups prepared mustard without thickeners
4 cups sugar
1 Tbsp. non-iodized salt
¾ cup Clear Jel
1 cup water

1. Stem peppers. Grind peppers with seeds.

2. Place in stockpot with vinegar, mustard, sugar, and salt. Stir together well.

3. Bring to simmer.

4. In small bowl, whisk Clear Jel and water together until smooth.

5. Stir into simmering pepper mixture.

6. Stir often until thickened, but do not boil.

7. Place in half-pint jars and process according to your canner's instructions.

Makes:

16 half-pints

Prep. Time:

30 minutes

Cooking Time:

15–20 minutes

Processing Time:

See your canner's manual

Pepper Butter is very common in our community. We use it mostly on sandwiches, but also with hard-boiled eggs, or spreading on meat at the table—especially sausage, hot dogs, and hamburgers. And yes, sometimes on crackers. I guess you could say it's a glorified mustard.

Spiced Peach Butter

10 lbs. peaches
1½ cups sugar
1½ tsp. cinnamon
1½ tsp. ginger
½ tsp. nutmeg
½ tsp. allspice

Makes:

3–4 pints

Prep. Time:

45 minutes

Cooking Time:

2–3 hours

Processing Time:

See your canner's manual

1. Peel peaches, pit, and chop. Place in large stockpot.

2. Stir in sugar and spices. Bring to boil.

3. Simmer uncovered for 2 to 3 hours, stirring occasionally.

4. Taste for sweetness and spice, adding more as desired.

5. When the fruit has broken down and the juices have thickened enough to coat a spoon, remove from heat. The butter will continue to thicken as it cools.

6. Keeps in jars in the fridge for several months, or can in pints following directions in your canner's manual.

Kitchen Stove Apple Butter

One cold winter day I put one quart of sweetened applesauce in a saucepan. I cooked it uncovered 3½-4 hours on low heat, stirring it occasionally, letting the scent cozy up the kitchen.

Once the sauce was cooked down and getting dark and thick, I added cinnamon to taste. We enjoyed it warm with fresh bread and butter. I stored the rest in the refrigerator.

Sour Cherry Jam

8 cups sour cherries, stemmed, pitted, and coarsely chopped
4 cups sugar
2 Tbsp. freshly squeezed lemon juice

1. Combine cherries, sugar, and lemon juice in a large heavy pot.

2. Bring to boil over medium heat, stirring constantly until sugar is dissolved.

3. Cook for about 30 minutes until the mixture thickens, stirring frequently.

4. Check for jelling. You can use a cooking thermometer to see if the jam has reached 220°, the jell point. Or dip a cold metal spoon in the hot jam and lift out a spoonful. As the drops of jam become heavier, finally two drops will stick together and then run slowly off the spoon like a sheet. That also indicates the jelling point. If it hasn't yet been reached, cook a few minutes longer and test again.

5. Skim off any foam that has developed.

6. Ladle into sterilized jars and process according to your canner's directions.

Makes:

4 half-pints

Prep. Time:

20 minutes

Cooking Time:

30–35 minutes

Processing Time:

See your canner's manual

Elderberry Jelly

2 cups elderberries, stripped off stems
¼ cup lemon juice
4½ cups sugar
1.75-oz. box pectin

1. Put elderberries in large saucepan. Cover with water.

2. Bring to boil and simmer 15 minutes.

3. Strain berries and liquid through cheesecloth. Mash berries to get out all liquid.

4. Measure out 3 cups of elderberry juice.

5. Follow directions on pectin box to make jelly.

6. Place in half-pint jars and process according to your canner's instructions.

Makes:

6 half-pints

Prep. Time:

20 minutes

Cooking Time:

25 minutes

Processing Time:

See your canner's manual

Canned Grape Juice

4 bunches Concord-type grapes, each containing at least 1 cup grapes
1⅓ cups sugar, *divided*
boiling water

1. Prepare 4 quart-size glass canning jars. Place 1 bunch grapes in each jar.

2. Place ⅓ cup sugar in each jar.

3. Fill each jar with boiling water. Add lids and rings. Process in canner according to your canner's directions.

Makes:

4 quarts

Prep. Time:

5 minutes

Cooking Time:

See your canner's manual

Raspberry Pie Filling

3 quarts (12 cups) raspberries
5 quarts (20 cups) water, *divided*

3½ cups Therm-Flo
8 cups sugar
½ tsp. salt

1. In a large pot, boil raspberries and 16 cups water for 10 minutes.

2. Mash through a strainer to remove seeds. Place seedless puree back in kettle.

3. In a bowl, mix Therm-Flo with remaining 4 cups water.

4. Add Therm-flo mixture, sugar, and salt to raspberry puree.

5. Cook over low heat, stirring constantly until mixture reaches a full boil and thickens.

6. Place in pint jars and process according to your canner's directions.

Makes:

15 pints

Prep. Time:

15 minutes

Cooking Time:

25 minutes

Processing Time:

See your canner's manual

One pint makes one 9" pie (not deep-dish).

Tomato Cocktail

1 peck (8 dry quarts) tomatoes
3-4 ribs celery with leaves included
1 bunch parsley
6 small onions
2 green bell peppers
1 cup sugar
¼ cup non-iodized salt
½ tsp. pepper

1. Cut up vegetables. Put in large stockpot.

2. Cook tomatoes, celery, parsley, onions, and bell peppers together until soft, stirring occasionally, 25-30 minutes.

3. Force mixture through sieve or food mill.

4. Add sugar, salt, and pepper to sieved mixture.

5. Put in jars and process according to your canner's directions.

Makes:

8-10 quarts

Prep. Time:

30 minutes

Cooking Time:

25-30 minutes

Processing Time:

See your canner's manual

This is delicious as a breakfast drink or to use in making chili.

The "FARM HOME" Cookbook

COOKIES

Chocolate Chip Peanut Butter Cookies

1 cup (2 sticks) butter, softened
1 cup peanut butter
1 cup brown sugar
1 cup sugar, plus more for rolling
2 eggs

3 cups all-purpose flour
1 cup dry rolled oats
2 tsp. baking soda
1 tsp. vanilla
½ tsp. salt
1 cup chocolate chips

Makes:

4 dozen

Prep. Time:

25 minutes

Chilling Time:

2-3 hours

Baking time:

10 minutes

1. Preheat oven to 350°.

2. Cream butter, peanut butter, sugars, and eggs together in mixing bowl.

3. Stir in rest of ingredients thoroughly.

4. Refrigerate for several hours.

5. Roll into balls 1½" in diameter. Put some sugar in a saucer. Roll the balls in sugar.

6. Lightly press flat on baking sheet, 2" apart from each other.

7. Bake in preheated oven until lightly brown, about 10 minutes.

Dipped Gingersnaps

1½ cups (3 sticks) butter
2 cups sugar, plus more for rolling
2 eggs
½ cup baking molasses *or* sorghum molasses
4 cups all-purpose flour
4 tsp. baking soda
1 tsp. ground ginger
2 tsp. cinnamon
1 tsp. salt
white chocolate, *or* white coating mix, for dipping

Makes:

4 dozen

Prep. Time:

25 minutes

Chilling Time:

30 minutes

Baking Time:

9-11 minutes

1. Preheat oven to 350°.

2. In a mixing bowl, cream butter and sugar together well. Add eggs and molasses. Beat again.

3. In a separate bowl, stir flour, baking soda, ginger, cinnamon, and salt together. Then add to wet ingredients. Mix well.

4. Chill dough in refrigerator for 30 minutes.

5. Shape into balls 1½" in diameter.

6. Put some sugar in a saucer. Roll the balls in sugar.

7. Space balls on baking sheets 2" apart.

8. Bake in preheated oven 9-11 minutes.

9. When cookies are cool, dip each one halfway into melted white chocolate or coating mix. Allow to harden before storing in a cookie tin.

Old-Fashioned Oatmeal Cookies

2 cups lard, *or* 1 cup lard and 1 cup (2 sticks) butter, softened
4 eggs
3 cups brown sugar
3 cups all-purpose flour
6 cups dry rolled oats
2 tsp. baking powder
2 tsp. vanilla
2 tsp. baking soda
1 tsp. salt
1½ cups chocolate *or* butterscotch chips, *optional*
confectioners sugar, for rolling

1. Preheat oven to 350°.

2. In a big mixing bowl, cream lard, eggs, and brown sugar together.

3. Stir in rest of ingredients except confectioners sugar.

4. Roll into balls, 1½" in diameter.

5. Put confectioners sugar on a saucer. Roll balls in sugar.

6. Put on baking sheet 2" apart. Press balls slightly flat.

7. Bake in preheated oven 15 minutes. Do not overbake.

Makes:

4–5 dozen

Prep. Time:

30 minutes

Baking Time:

15 minutes

Note:

For a softer cookie, remove from oven when there is still a slight indentation in the center of the cookie, after about 13 minutes of baking. Leave on baking sheet for several minutes after removing from oven.

Frosted Date Cookies

¾ cup (1½ sticks) butter, softened, *divided*
2¼ cups all-purpose flour
1¼ cups brown sugar
1 tsp. vanilla
2 eggs, beaten
½ cup sour cream
½ tsp. baking soda
1 cup chopped nuts
½ tsp. salt
1 cup finely chopped dried dates
1½ cups confectioners sugar
3-4 Tbsp. hot water
¼ tsp. vanilla

Makes:

3 dozen

Prep. Time:

25 minutes

Baking Time:

8-10 minutes

1. Preheat oven to 375°.

2. In mixing bowl, in order given, mix together well ½ cup butter, flour, brown sugar, vanilla, eggs, sour cream, baking soda, nuts, salt, and dates.

3. Drop by teaspoonsful onto baking sheets, 2" apart.

4. Bake in preheated oven 8-10 minutes.

5. Cool before frosting.

6. To make frosting, place remaining ¼ cup butter in saucepan. Melt over low heat until it turns brown. ALERT: watch closely and take off heat as it gets toasty brown and smells nutty. It can easily burn.

7. Stir confectioners sugar, hot water, and vanilla into brown butter, beating until smooth.

8. Spread cookies with frosting.

Dig out an apron and discover how useful it can be! (Thanks to a friend who found this.)

- The principal use of Grandma's apron was to protect her dress, but along with that, it served as a potholder for removing hot pans from the oven.

- It was wonderful for drying children's tears, and on occasion was even used for cleaning out dirty ears.

- From the chicken coop, she used her apron for carrying eggs, fussy chicks, and sometimes half-hatched eggs to be finished in the warming oven.

- When company came, her shy kids hid in its folds.

- When the weather was cold, Grandma wrapped it around her arms.

- Those big old aprons wiped many perspiring foreheads, bent over the hot stove.

- She brought chips and kindling into the kitchen in that apron.

- From the garden, she carried all sorts of vegetables. After the peas had been shelled, it carried out the hulls.

- In the fall, she used her apron to bring in apples that had fallen from the trees.

- When unexpected company drove up the road, it was surprising how much furniture that old apron could dust in a matter of seconds.

- When dinner was ready, Grandma walked out onto the porch and waved her apron, and the men knew it was time to come in from the fields for dinner.

It will be a long time before anyone invents
something as versatile as that apron.

Thumbprint Cookies

1 cup (2 sticks) butter, softened
½ cup brown sugar
2 egg yolks
1 tsp. vanilla
2 cups all-purpose flour
½ tsp. salt
2 egg whites
finely chopped nuts
Cream Cheese Frosting (see recipe on pages 196-197)
   or jam, for filling

Makes:
_____
2 dozen

Prep. Time:
_____
20 minutes

Baking Time:
_____
10-12 minutes

1. Preheat oven to 400°.

2. Cream butter, sugar, egg yolks, and vanilla thoroughly in a mixing bowl.

3. Stir in flour and salt thoroughly.

4. Roll 1 tsp. dough into a ball. Continue with all of dough.

5. Dip each ball in slightly beaten egg whites, then roll in nuts.

6. Place balls 1" apart on ungreased baking sheet. Press thumb gently into center to make a little hollow.

7. Bake in preheated oven for 10-12 minutes.

8. Cool cookies on cooling rack. When cool, fill centers with Cream Cheese Frosting or jam.

Snow Drops

2¼ cups all-purpose flour
¼ tsp. salt
1 cup (2 sticks) butter, room temperature
¾ cup sifted confectioners sugar, *divided*
1 tsp. vanilla
¾ cup finely chopped hickory nuts *or* walnuts

1. Preheat oven to 400°.

2. Combine flour and salt. Set aside.

3. Cream butter, ½ cup sugar, and vanilla together.

4. Add dry ingredients and nuts to creamed ingredients, mixing thoroughly.

5. Chill dough for 1 hour.

6. Form into balls 1" in diameter. Place balls 1" apart on ungreased baking sheet.

7. Bake in preheated oven 10-12 minutes.

8. While still warm, roll cookies in remaining ¼ cup confectioners sugar. Cool. Roll in sugar again.

Makes:

about 2 dozen

Prep. Time:

15 minutes

Chilling Time:

1 hour

Baking Time:

10-12 minutes

We make these
at Christmas time.

Very Blueberry Bars

1 cup (2 sticks) butter,
softened
1½ cups sugar
4 eggs
1 tsp. vanilla
1 tsp. almond flavoring
3 cups + 1 Tbsp. all-purpose
flour, *divided*

½ tsp. baking powder
3 tsp. cornstarch
4 cups fresh *or* frozen
blueberries, *divided*
2 tsp. lemon juice, *divided*
1 cup confectioners sugar
1 Tbsp. milk

Makes:

15 servings

Prep. Time:

25 minutes

Baking Time:

35 minutes

1. Preheat oven to 350°.

2. Make batter by beating together butter, sugar, eggs, vanilla, and almond flavoring in mixing bowl.

3. Stir in 3 cups flour and baking powder.

4. Spread ⅔ of batter in greased 9" × 13" baking pan. Set aside.

5. In another mixing bowl, combine remaining 1 Tbsp. flour and cornstarch.

6. Add ½ cup blueberries and 1 tsp. lemon juice to dry ingredients. Mash with fork and mix.

7. Add remaining berries. Stir gently to coat.

8. Pour berry mixture over batter in baking pan.

9. Dollop remaining batter by tablespoonsful on top. Berries will show through.

10. Bake in preheated oven 35 minutes, or until golden.

11. Mix confectioners sugar, remaining 1 tsp. lemon juice, and milk to make glaze. Drizzle over baked bars.

12. Cut bars when cooled to room temperature.

Rocky Road Candy Bars

6–8 whole graham crackers
2 cups miniature marshmallows
½ cup (1 stick) butter, cut into thin slices
1 cup confectioners sugar
1 egg, beaten
6 oz. chocolate chips

1. Line an 8" × 8" baking pan with whole graham crackers.

2. Sprinkle with mini marshmallows. Set aside.

3. Fill bottom of double boiler half-full with water. In top of double boiler, stir together butter, confectioners sugar, egg, and chocolate chips over medium heat. (Be sure that water in the bottom pan does not touch the top part of the double boiler.)

4. When chocolate mixture is melted and thoroughly combined, pour it over graham crackers and marshmallows in pan.

5. Cut when thoroughly cool.

Makes:

16 bars

Prep. Time:

10 minutes

Cooking Time:

10 minutes

Variation:

Use butterscotch chips instead of chocolate.

Later this week I'll be helping our neighbor do six bushels of pears. The family has five boys who helped us out quite often this summer when we had hay to bale. Good neighbors are such a blessing, and we surely have good ones around here.

Pear Bars

⅓ cup (5⅓ Tbsp.) butter, softened
⅓ cup brown sugar
¾ cup all-purpose flour
¼ tsp. salt
⅔ cup chopped nuts
8 oz. cream cheese, (see recipe on page 273) room temperature
½ cup + 1 tsp. sugar, *divided*
½ tsp. vanilla
1 egg
3 cups fresh, peeled and sliced pears
½ tsp. cinnamon

1. Preheat oven to 350°.

2. In mixing bowl, cream together butter and brown sugar.

3. Beat in flour and salt.

4. Stir in nuts. Press into greased 8" × 8" baking pan.

5. Bake in preheated oven 20 minutes, or until lightly browned.

6. Cool in pan on wire rack.

7. In mixing bowl, beat cream cheese until smooth.

8. Mix in ½ cup sugar, vanilla, and egg. Pour over crust.

9. Arrange pear slices over filling. Sprinkle with remaining 1 tsp. sugar and cinnamon.

10. Bake in preheated oven 25-30 minutes. Center will be soft and will become firmer upon cooling.

11. Cool 45 minutes, then cover and refrigerate at least 45 minutes before cutting. Store in fridge.

Makes:

16 bars

Prep. Time:

30 minutes

Cooling/Chilling Time:

2 hours

Baking time:

45-50 minutes

Variation:

Use 1 cup yogurt in place of the cream cheese. No need to beat it.

Sour Cream Rhubarb Squares

1 cup (2 sticks) butter,
   softened
1½ cups brown sugar, *divided*
1¾ cups all-purpose flour
2 cups dry rolled oats
1 tsp. baking powder
1 tsp. baking soda

½ tsp. salt
4 egg yolks
2 Tbsp. Clear Jel *or* cornstarch
2 cups chopped rhubarb
½ cup sugar
2 cups sour cream

Makes:

15–18 servings

Prep. Time:

30 minutes

Cooling Time:

10–15 minutes

Baking Time:

30 minutes

1. Preheat oven to 350°.

2. In a mixing bowl, cream butter and 1 cup brown sugar together.

3. Mix in flour, oats, baking powder, baking soda, and salt. Mixture will be crumbly.

4. Set aside 2 cups of the crumbs.

5. Pat remaining crumbs into a greased 9" × 13" baking pan.

6. Bake in preheated oven 15 minutes. Set aside to cool while you make the filling.

7. Combine rest of ingredients, including ½ cup brown sugar, in saucepan, whisking until well mixed.

8. Bring to a boil and cook, stirring constantly for 5 minutes.

9. Pour over crust. Sprinkle with reserved crumbs.

10. Return to preheated oven for 15 minutes.

11. Cool thoroughly before cutting into squares to serve.

The "Farm Home" Cookbook

CAKES

Favorite Chocolate Cake

¾ cup (1½ sticks) butter, room temperature

2 cups sugar

2 eggs

2½ cups all-purpose flour

½ cup unsweetened cocoa powder

1 cup sour milk* or buttermilk

¼ tsp. salt

1 tsp. vanilla

2 tsp. baking soda

1 cup boiling water

Make sour milk by placing 2 Tbsp. vinegar into a one-cup measure. Fill the cup with milk. Let stand 2-3 minutes. Stir and use.

Makes:

12-16 servings

Prep. Time:

20 minutes

Baking Time:

45 minutes

1. Preheat oven to 350°.

2. In a mixing bowl, cream together butter and sugar. Add eggs and beat well.

3. In a separate bowl, stir together flour and cocoa powder. Add alternately with sour milk to creamed ingredients, beating after each addition.

4. Stir in salt and vanilla.

5. In a small bowl, dissolve soda in boiling water. Mix into batter.

6. Pour batter into greased 9" × 13" baking pan.

7. Bake in preheated oven 45 minutes, or until tester inserted in middle of cake comes out clean.

This is our all-time favorite chocolate cake. We love it with chocolate or caramel frosting.

Hot Fudge Cake

1 cup all-purpose flour
¾ cup sugar
6 Tbsp. unsweetened cocoa powder, *divided*
2 tsp. baking powder
¼ tsp. salt
½ cup milk
2 Tbsp. (¼ stick) butter, melted
1 tsp. vanilla
1 cup brown sugar
1¼ cups hot water

1. Preheat oven to 350°.

2. In a mixing bowl, combine in this order: flour, sugar, 2 Tbsp. cocoa, baking powder, salt, milk, butter, and vanilla. Mix well.

3. Pour into a 9" × 13" baking pan.

4. Stir together brown sugar and remaining 4 Tbsp. cocoa powder.

5. Sprinkle brown sugar mixture on top of cake batter, then pour hot water over everything. Do NOT stir!

6. Bake in preheated oven 40 minutes.

Makes:

12 servings

Prep. Time:

10 minutes

Baking Time:

40 minutes

Note:

The cake will float on top of hot fudge sauce when it's done. Serve while warm with milk or ice cream.

Apple Cinnamon Cake with Hot Butter Sauce

2 eggs

1 cup sugar

¾ cup (1½ sticks) butter, softened

5 medium apples, peeled and shredded

1 tsp. baking soda

1 tsp. baking powder

1½ tsp. cinnamon

½ tsp. salt

½ cup chopped nuts, optional

1½ cups all-purpose flour

Hot Butter Sauce

½ cup (1 stick) butter

1 cup brown sugar

½ cup heavy cream

2 tsp. vanilla

vanilla ice cream, for serving

Makes:

12-15 servings

Prep. Time:

25 minutes

Baking Time:

40 minutes

Note:

You can also serve maple nut or butter pecan ice cream instead of vanilla.

1. Preheat oven to 325°.

2. In a mixing bowl, beat together eggs, sugar, and butter.

3. Stir in apples, baking soda, baking powder, cinnamon, salt, nuts, and flour. Stir until well mixed.

4. Pour into greased and floured 10" × 15" baking pan.

5. Bake in preheated oven 40 minutes, or until center is firm to touch.

6. Combine Hot Butter Sauce ingredients in saucepan. When butter melts, stir until well blended.

7. Heat slowly over low heat until thickened.

8. To serve each person, put a slice of cake on a dessert plate. Add a scoop of ice cream, then pour Hot Butter Sauce over all.

A very snazzy and delicious dessert.

Lemon Pudding Cake

½ cup all-purpose flour
1½ cups sugar, *divided*
¾ tsp. baking powder
¼ tsp. salt
3 eggs, separated
2 Tbsp. (¼ stick) butter, melted
juice of 1 large lemon
grated zest of 1 large lemon
1½ cups milk
whipped cream, for serving

Makes:

8-10 servings

Prep. Time:

25 minutes

Baking Time:

45 minutes

1. Preheat oven to 350°.

2. Combine flour, 1 cup sugar, baking powder, and salt in mixing bowl.

3. In a separate bowl, beat egg whites with ½ cup sugar until stiff and glossy.

4. In another bowl, beat egg yolks with melted butter, lemon juice, lemon zest, and milk.

5. Pour this mixture over combined dry ingredients, mixing well. Fold in beaten egg whites.

6. Pour into buttered 8" × 8" baking dish.

7. Place filled baking dish in a larger pan, such as a 9" × 13", with a half-inch of hot water in it.

8. Bake in preheated oven 45 minutes. The top will be puffy and lightly browned, and the bottom will be saucy.

9. Remove 8" × 8" pan from larger pan to cool. Serve garnished with whipped cream.

Farm Stand Carrot Cake with Cream Cheese Frosting

2 cups all-purpose flour
2 cups sugar
1 Tbsp. cinnamon
2 tsp. baking powder
2 tsp. baking soda
1 tsp. salt
4 eggs
1½ cups (3 sticks) melted butter
2 tsp. vanilla
3 cups grated carrots, packed
1 cup chopped walnuts *or* pecans

Cream Cheese Frosting:
8 oz. cream cheese, softened
½ cup (1 stick) butter, softened
4 cups confectioners sugar, sifted, *divided*
1 Tbsp. vanilla
1 Tbsp. milk *or* water, if needed
2 cups chopped walnuts *or* pecans

Makes:

20 servings

Prep. Time:

60 minutes

Baking Time:

60 minutes

Variation:

Instead of making a layer cake, bake batter in a 9" × 13" baking pan. Halve the frosting recipe if you do that.

1. Preheat oven to 325°.

2. Heavily butter and flour two round 9" cake pans. Set aside.

3. Combine flour, sugar, cinnamon, baking powder, baking soda, and salt in large bowl.

4. In small bowl, whisk together eggs, melted butter, and vanilla.

5. Add egg mixture to flour mixture. Stir to combine.

6. Add carrots and nuts. Stir to combine.

7. Evenly divide batter between two prepared cake pans.

8. Bake in preheated oven 55–65 minutes, until tester inserted in middle comes out clean.

9. Let cake cool in pans completely, about one hour.

10. Make frosting in mixing bowl by beating cream cheese and butter together until smooth and creamy.

11. Add 3½ cups confectioners sugar gradually, beating until it is fully incorporated and smooth.

12. Stir in vanilla. If frosting is too soft, add remaining confectioners sugar. If it is too stiff, add milk or water.

13. Run a knife around edge of each cake layer to loosen it from pan. Invert to unmold.

14. Place one layer on plate. Spread some frosting on top, covering to edges. Place second layer on top of frosting. Frost sides and top of cake.

15. Press 2 cups nuts onto side of cake.

Hickory Nut Cake with Caramel Frosting

3 cups cake flour (see recipe
   on page 270)
3 tsp. baking powder
½ tsp. salt
1 cup (2 sticks) butter, softened
2 cups sugar
1 cup cold water
6 egg whites
1 tsp. vanilla extract
1 cup chopped hickory nuts

Caramel Frosting:
4 cups confectioners sugar
⅔ (10⅔ Tbps.) cup butter
2 cups brown sugar, packed
½ cup milk
4 marshmallows, regular size,
   or 40 miniatures
3 tsp. vanilla extract

Makes:

12-16 servings

Prep. Time:

50 minutes

Baking Time:

30 minutes

1. Preheat oven to 350°.

2. Sift flour, baking powder, and salt together. Set aside.

3. In large mixing bowl, cream butter and sugar until light and fluffy.

4. Blend water alternately with flour mixture into butter mixture.

5. Separately, beat egg whites until they hold stiff peaks. Beat vanilla into egg whites.

6. Fold beaten egg whites into cake batter. Gradually fold in nuts.

7. Pour into 3 greased 8" cake pans.

8. Bake in preheated oven 30 minutes, or until cake tester inserted in center of cake layers comes out clean. Allow to stand a few minutes before removing from pans.

9. When cool, make Caramel Frosting.

10. Sift confectioners sugar into a small bowl and set aside.

11. In medium saucepan, melt butter and then stir in brown sugar.

12. Stir in milk until blended. Stir in marshmallows. Bring to boil over low heat.

13. Cook two minutes, stirring constantly.

14. Remove from heat. Stir in confectioners sugar and vanilla extract. Beat until smooth and creamy. If frosting is too thick, beat in ½ tsp. milk at a time until it reaches desired consistency.

15. Place one cake layer on a plate. Spread frosting over top to edges. Place second cake layer on top and repeat frosting for this and final layer.

16. Frost sides and top of cake.

We have hickory trees in several of our fencerows, and we gather nuts every fall. One of the trees is young, and its nuts are larger than most and not as prone to being parasitized by grubs. Hickory trees can be up to a hundred years old and are considered a very desirable tree.

You probably won't find any hickory nuts in stores because the nuts are small, take lots of time to crack, and even then it is tedious to pick out the little pieces of the shell that inevitably end up with the nut meats.

Cracking hickory nuts is something elderly people or someone who cannot get around too well, especially men, often do in our community. Sometimes we sit around the table cracking nuts, making it a family affair. The grandchildren love to help (and eat). Hickory nuts taste very similar to pecans, so if you don't have hickory trees and time to crack the nuts, just substitute pecans.

Blueberry Supper Cake

2 cups all-purpose flour
1½ cups sugar
⅔ cup (10⅔ Tbsp.) butter
2 tsp. baking powder

1 tsp. salt
2 eggs, separated
1 cup milk
2 cups blueberries

Makes:

15–18 servings

Prep. Time:

20 minutes

Baking Time:

35–40 minutes

Note:

Delicious served warm with milk or as a dessert with ice cream.

1. Preheat oven to 350°.

2. Place flour and sugar in mixing bowl. Cut in butter to make crumbs, using pastry cutter or two knives. When crumbs form, remove 1 cup and set aside.

3. To rest of crumbs, add baking powder, salt, 2 egg yolks, and milk.

4. In a separate bowl, beat 2 egg whites until stiff. Fold into batter.

5. Grease 9" × 13" baking pan. Pour in batter.

6. Sprinkle blueberries over top.

7. Sprinkle reserved 1 cup crumbs over blueberries.

8. Bake in preheated oven until golden brown, 35–40 minutes.

Toffee Nutmeg Cake

3 cups all-purpose flour
2 cups brown sugar
1 tsp. baking powder
½ tsp. salt
¾ cup (1½ sticks) butter, softened
½ cup finely chopped pecans
1 egg, lightly beaten
2-3 tsp. ground nutmeg
1½ tsp. vanilla
1½ cups sour cream
1½ tsp. baking soda
¾ cup coarsely chopped pecans

Makes:

15-20 servings

Prep. Time:

30 minutes

Baking Time:

1 hour

Cooling Time:

15 minutes

Tip:

Serve with butter pecan ice cream or whipped cream.

1. Preheat oven to 350°.

2. Grease and lightly flour a 9"- or 10"-tube pan with a removable bottom. Set aside.

3. In large bowl, using a pastry blender, combine flour, brown sugar, baking powder, and salt.

4. Then cut in butter until mixture is crumbly.

5. Combine 3 cups of this mixture with ½ cup finely chopped pecans. Place in bottom of tube pan.

6. Into remaining mixture stir egg, nutmeg, and vanilla.

7. In separate bowl, combine sour cream and baking soda. Add to mixture along with ¾ cup coarsely chopped pecans.

8. Pour over flour mixture in tube pan.

9. Bake 1 hour in preheated oven, or until cake tester comes out clean. Cool on wire rack 15 minutes. Remove sides of pan and cool completely.

10. Invert onto serving plate.

Gingerbread

½ cup (1 stick) butter, room temperature
½ cup sugar
1 cup sorghum molasses *or* mild baking molasses
1 egg, beaten
1½ tsp. baking soda
1 tsp. ginger
1 tsp. cinnamon
½ tsp. ground cloves
½ tsp. salt
2½ cups all-purpose flour
1 cup hot coffee
whipped cream, for serving

Makes:

12–15 servings

Prep. Time:

20 minutes

Baking Time:

35 minutes

1. Preheat oven to 350°.

2. In mixing bowl, cream butter. Add sugar. Cream well.

3. Add molasses and egg. Mix well.

4. In a separate bowl, mix together baking soda, ginger, cinnamon, ground cloves, salt, and flour. Stir into wet ingredients.

5. Add hot coffee. Stir.

6. Pour batter into a 9" × 13" baking pan.

7. Bake in preheated oven 35 minutes, or until toothpick inserted in center comes out clean.

8. Serve warm with whipped cream.

Oatmeal Cake

1 cup dry rolled oats
½ cup (1 stick) butter, cut into
   slices
1¼ cups boiling water
2 eggs
1½ cups all-purpose flour
1 cup brown sugar
¾ cup sugar
1 tsp. baking soda
1 tsp. cinnamon
½ tsp. salt
1 tsp. vanilla

Topping:
¼ cup (half stick) butter
¾ cup brown sugar
6 Tbsp. cream or half-and-
   half
¾ cup chopped nuts of your
   choice

Makes:

10-12 servings

Prep. Time:

15 minutes

Standing Time:

30 minutes

Baking/Cooking Time:

1 hour

1. Preheat oven to 350°.

2. In large, heat-proof mixing bowl, pour boiling water over rolled oats and butter slices. Stir, then let stand 20 minutes.

3. Beat eggs into cooled oats mixture.

4. Add rest of ingredients. Stir.

5. Pour into greased and floured 9" × 13" baking pan.

6. Bake in preheated oven 40-45 minutes, or until tester inserted in middle comes out clean.

7. Make topping by melting butter in small saucepan.

8. Stir in sugar and cream.

9. Turn heat to low and cook 3 minutes, stirring often.

10. Take off heat and let cool 10 minutes. Stir in nuts.

11. Pour topping over warm cake, using a table knife to spread evenly.

Spice Cake Roll

3 eggs
½ cup maple syrup
1 cup buttermilk
1 tsp. lemon juice
1½ cups whole wheat pastry
   flour *or* all-purpose flour
1 tsp. baking powder
1 tsp. cinnamon
½ tsp. ginger
½ tsp. nutmeg
½ tsp. salt
confectioners sugar, for
   rolling

Filling:
8 oz. cream cheese, softened
   (see recipe on page 273)
½ cup maple syrup
2 tsp. vanilla
2 Tbsp. (¼ stick) butter,
   softened

Makes:
_____
10-12 servings

Prep. Time:
_____
20 minutes

Cooling Time:
_____
1 hour

Baking Time:
_____
15 minutes

1. Preheat oven to 375°.

2. In mixing bowl, beat eggs until thick and lemon-colored.

3. Add maple syrup, buttermilk, lemon juice, flour, baking powder, spices, and salt. Fold together gently.

4. Spread batter in greased and floured 10" × 15" baking pan.

5. Bake in preheated oven 15 minutes.

6. Let cake cool 5 minutes. Then loosen around edges and turn cake out onto a linen kitchen towel which has been lightly dusted with confectioners sugar.

7. Roll up towel and cake together, starting with a short side. Allow to cool rolled up, about 1 hour.

8. In mixing bowl, beat filling ingredients together well.

9. Unroll cake. Remove towel. Spread filling on cake.

10. Roll cake back up and chill before serving.

Great-Grandma's Crumb Cake

1¾ cups brown sugar
½ cup lard, at room temperature
2½ cups all-purpose flour

1 cup buttermilk
1½ tsp. baking soda
2 eggs
1 tsp. vanilla

Makes:

12–15 servings

Prep. Time:

10 minutes

Baking Time:

25 minutes

1. Preheat oven to 350°.

2. In mixing bowl, cream brown sugar and lard together.

3. Remove and reserve 1 cup crumbs.

4. Add rest of ingredients to mixing bowl and stir to combine.

5. Pour batter in lightly greased 9" × 13" baking pan. Sprinkle with reserved crumbs.

6. Bake in preheated oven until lightly browned, about 25 minutes.

I got this recipe from Charlene Stoller, who said her great-grandma served this cake with fresh strawberries or peaches in the summer.

Creamy Cocoa Frosting

2¾ cups sifted confectioners sugar
⅓ cup unsweetened cocoa powder
⅓ cup (5⅓ Tbsp.) butter, room temperature
3–4 Tbsp. milk

Makes:

enough for two 8" or 9" layers, or a 9" × 13" cake

Prep. Time:

5 minutes

1. In mixing bowl, sift sugar and cocoa together.

2. Add butter and milk.

3. Stir until well blended.

Easy Penuche Frosting

½ cup (1 stick) butter
1 cup brown sugar
¼ cup milk
1¾ –2 cups sifted confectioners sugar

1. Melt butter in saucepan. Stir in brown sugar.

2. Boil and stir over low heat for 2 minutes.

3. Stir in milk. Bring to boil again, stirring constantly.

4. Cool to lukewarm. Then gradually stir in confectioners sugar.

5. Place pan in ice water and stir until thick enough to spread.

Makes:

enough for two 8"
or 9" layers, or a
9" × 13" cake

Prep. Time:

10 minutes

Coconut Pecan Frosting

1 cup heavy cream
1 cup sugar
3 egg yolks
½ cup (1 stick) butter
1 tsp. vanilla
1½ cups shredded coconut
1 cup chopped pecans

Delicious on any cake!

1. Boil cream, sugar, egg yolks, and butter for 12 minutes on low heat.

2. Let cool for 15 minutes, then stir in rest of ingredients.

Makes:

enough for two 8"
or 9" layers, or a
9" × 13" cake

Prep. Time:

15 minutes

Cooling Time:

15 minutes

The "Farm Home" Cookbook

PIES

Sour Cherry Pie

1 pint canned sour cherries, including juice
¾ cup sugar
¼ tsp. salt
3 tsp. Clear Jel
¾ cup water
2 Tbsp. (¼ stick) butter
9" unbaked pie shell (see recipe on page 220)
1 recipe Crumb Topping (see recipe on page 211)

1. Preheat oven to 375°.

2. Put cherries with juice, salt, and sugar into saucepan. Bring almost to boiling.

3. Separately, dissolve Clear Jel in water. Stir into hot cherries.

4. Keep on stirring gently until mixture boils. Boil for 1 minute.

5. Remove from heat. Add butter to hot cherries.

6. Pour filling in pie shell. Top with Crumb Topping.

7. Bake in preheated oven 35-40 minutes, until filling bubbles at edges and crumbs are browned. Cool before serving.

Makes:

a 9" pie

Prep. Time:

20 minutes

Cooking/Baking Time:

35-40 minutes

Variation:

Use a double crust instead of crumbs. Bake the same way.

Famous Lemon Pie

3 heaping Tbsp. cornstarch

1 cup sugar

⅓ cup fresh lemon juice

1 Tbsp. grated lemon rind

3 eggs, separated

1½ cups boiling water

2 Tbsp. (¼ stick) butter, at
  room temperature

¼ cup heavy cream

2 tsp. lemon extract, *optional*

9" baked pie shell (see recipes
  on pages 220 and 217)

Meringue:

3 egg whites reserved from
  filling recipe

¼ tsp. cream of tartar

5 Tbsp. sugar

1 tsp. cornstarch

1 Tbsp. vanilla

Makes:

a 9" pie

Prep. Time:

30 minutes

Cooking/Baking Time:

20-25 minutes

Chilling Time:

at least 2 hours

1. Preheat oven to 400°.

2. In saucepan, combine cornstarch, sugar, lemon juice, and lemon rind.

3. Beat egg yolks in separate bowl. (Reserve egg whites.) Then add to cornstarch mixture.

4. Gradually add boiling water while whisking constantly. Turn on heat, and boil 4 minutes, continuing to whisk constantly.

5. Remove from heat. Add butter and cream. Add lemon extract if desired.

6. Pour hot filling into baked pie shell.

7. To make meringue, beat egg whites and cream of tartar together until soft peaks form.

8. In separate bowl, mix sugar and cornstarch together. Then beat into egg whites, 1 Tbsp. at a time.

9. Add vanilla to mixture and beat until stiff.

10. Spread meringue over pie, sealing edges well, then use spoon to pull meringue into peaks and tips.

11. Bake in preheated oven 8-10 minutes, or until delicately browned.

12. Cool. Then chill before serving.

Best Berry and Peach Pie

4 cups blueberries, raspberries, *or*
blackberries, *or* a combination
1 ripe peach *or* nectarine, peeled
and sliced
½ cup sugar
1½ Tbsp. all-purpose flour

1 tsp. lemon zest
¼ tsp. vanilla extract
unbaked 9" pie shell
and crust for top (see
recipes on page 220)
1 egg, beaten, *optional*

Makes:

a 9" double-crust
pie

Prep. Time:

10 minutes

Baking Time:

50–52 minutes

Cooling Time:

1–2 hours

1. Preheat oven to 375°.

2. Gently mix berries, peach slices, sugar, flour, lemon zest, and vanilla extract together until fruit is well coated.

3. Pour into pie shell. Add pie dough strips on top of pie filling, creating a crisscross lattice pattern.

4. Brush lattice and edge of bottom crust with beaten egg, if desired.

5. Bake in preheated oven 40 minutes. Then reduce heat to 325° and bake another 10–12 minutes, until juices are bubbling and crust is nicely browned. Cool before serving.

Fresh Apple Pie

3 cups peeled apples, diced *or* sliced
⅔ cup sugar
1 Tbsp. all-purpose flour
½ tsp. cinnamon
9" unbaked pie shell and top crust (see recipes on page 220)
2 Tbsp. heavy cream
2 Tbsp. (¼ stick) butter, melted

1. Preheat oven to 375°.

2. Mix apples, sugar, flour, and cinnamon together. Pour into unbaked pie crust.

3. Top with cream and butter.

4. Cover with top crust or strips.

5. Bake in preheated oven 50 minutes, or until apples are soft and juices are bubbling. Cool before serving.

Makes:

a 9" pie

Prep. Time:

15 minutes

Baking Time:

50 minutes

Cooling Time:

1-2 hours

Variation:

Top with crumbs instead of a crust. See Crumb Topping recipe below.

Crumb Topping

1 cup brown sugar
1½ cups all-purpose flour
1½ cups dry rolled oats
¾ cup (1½ sticks) butter, at room temperature

1. Mix all together with pastry blender.

2. Store in freezer in airtight container.

3. Use generous one cup per pie topping.

Makes:

about 4 cups

Prep. Time:

15 minutes

Note:

This is enough crumbs to top 3-4 pies.

Blueberry Pie

1 egg
1 cup sugar
¼ cup all-purpose flour,
  divided
½ tsp. vanilla
1 cup sour cream
¼ tsp. salt

2 cups blueberries
9" unbaked pie shell (see
  recipes on page 220)
1½ Tbsp. butter, at room
  temperature
½ cup chopped pecans

Makes:

a 9" pie

Prep. Time:

15 minutes

Baking Time:

50 minutes

1. Preheat oven to 350°.

2. In bowl, mix together egg, sugar, 2 Tbsp. flour, vanilla, sour cream, and salt.

3. Fold in blueberries. Pour into pie shell.

4. Bake 30 minutes preheated oven.

5. While pie is baking, mix topping: butter, remaining 2 Tbsp. flour, and pecans. When pie has baked 30 minutes, sprinkle topping over blueberries. Return to oven to bake 20 more minutes.

6. Cool before serving.

Rhubarb Crumb Pie

3 cups diced rhubarb

2 Tbsp. all-purpose flour

1½ cups sugar

2 eggs

9" unbaked pie shell (see recipes on page 220)

1¼ cups Crumb Topping (see recipe on page 211)

1. Preheat oven to 425°.

2. Combine rhubarb with 2 Tbsp. flour and sugar in bowl.

3. Beat eggs in separate bowl and add to mixture.

4. Spread into a 9" unbaked pie shell.

5. Make Crumbs from recipe on page 211. Sprinkle on top of rhubarb mixture.

6. Bake in preheated oven 10 minutes. Reduce heat to 300° and bake 30 minutes more, until set in the middle. Cool before serving.

Makes:

a 9" pie

Prep. Time:

15 minutes

Baking Time:

40 minutes

Cooling Time:

1-2 hours

I have a perennial flowerbed in perfect view through my kitchen window. We planted most of the flowers especially to attract butterflies. Our lily-growing veterinarian gave David a tall Gold Eagle lily bulb several years ago. We planted it in this flowerbed, and because it is so tall, David set in a metal post and put a bluebird house on top, providing the support the lily needed. The other morning I heard the cheerful song of a bluebird, so I stepped outside—and there he was—on top of that birdhouse singing his heart out. His mate was perched on the apple tree nearby. Dare I hope they will nest there beside the Gold Eagle?

Grape Pie

3 cups Concord-type grapes, pinched out of skins, skins saved
1½ cups sugar, *divided*
3 Tbsp. + 1 cup all-purpose flour, *divided*
1 Tbsp. lemon juice
9" unbaked pie shell (see recipes on page 220)
¼ cup (half stick) butter, room temperature

Makes:

a 9" pie

Prep. Time:

35 minutes

Baking Time:

40 minutes

1. Preheat oven to 425°.

2. In saucepan, simmer grape pulp uncovered 5 minutes.

3. Press hot pulp through sieve to remove seeds.

4. Combine pulp and reserved skins in good-sized bowl.

5. Stir 1 cup sugar, 3 Tbsp. flour, and lemon juice into grapes.

6. Pour into pastry shell.

7. Make crumbs by combining remaining 1 cup flour, remaining ½ cup sugar, and butter.

8. Sprinkle over grape filling.

9. Bake in preheated oven 10 minutes. Reduce heat to 350° and bake 30 minutes more, until bubbling at edges.

Pecan Pie

3 eggs
½ cup sour cream
½ cup maple syrup
¾ cup brown sugar
1 tsp. vanilla

¼ tsp. salt
2 Tbsp. (¼ stick) butter, melted
1 cup chopped pecans
9" unbaked pie shell (see recipes
    on page 220)

Makes:

a 9" pie

Prep. Time:

15 minutes

Baking Time:

45–50 minutes

Cooking Time:

1–2 hours

1. Preheat oven to 425°.

2. Beat eggs in bowl. Add sour cream, maple syrup, and brown sugar. Whisk until smooth.

3. Stir in vanilla, salt, butter, and pecans. Pour into pie shell.

4. Bake in preheated oven 10 minutes. Reduce heat to 350°. Bake 35–40 minutes more, until set in the middle. Cool before serving.

This baked pie can be frozen to have on hand for a convenient dessert. Simply thaw before eating.

Pumpkin Pie

5 eggs, separated
½ tsp. salt
½ cup brown sugar
1 cup sugar
2½ Tbsp. all-purpose flour
2 cups cooked, pureed pumpkin;
   plain canned pumpkin is fine

1½ tsp. cinnamon
½ tsp. ground cloves
½ tsp. ginger
3½ cups half-and-half
two 10" unbaked pie shells
   (see recipes on page 220)

Makes:

two 10" pies

Prep. Time:

25 minutes

Baking Time:

35–40 minutes

Cooling Times:

1–2 hours

1. Preheat oven to 425°.

2. In a small bowl, beat egg whites; set aside.

3. In a larger bowl, beat egg yolks. Then add salt, brown sugar, sugar, flour, pumpkin, cinnamon, ground cloves, and ginger, beating well.

4. Heat half-and-half until steaming. Stir hot half-and-half into pumpkin mixture.

5. Fold in beaten egg whites.

6. Pour into two pie shells.

7. Bake in preheated oven 10 minutes. Then reduce oven temperature to 350° and bake 25–30 minutes longer until set in the middle. Cool before slicing.

I like to make this into two 8" pies, plus a little 6" pie, for our grandchildren or bachelor-neighbor.

Sour Cream Raisin Pie

¾ cup raisins
½ cup water
¾ cup sugar, *divided*
1¾ cups milk, *divided*
3 Tbsp. cornstarch
3 egg yolks
¼ tsp. salt

¾ cup sour cream
1 tsp. vanilla
1 Tbsp. lemon juice
9" baked pie shell (see
    recipes on page 220)
whipped cream

Makes:

a 9" pie

Prep. Time:

20 minutes

Cooking Time:

20 minutes

Cooling Time:

1–2 hours

1. In small saucepan, boil raisins and water together until raisins are soft, about 5 minutes. Set aside.

2. In larger saucepan, stir ½ cup sugar into 1½ cups milk. Bring to boil.

3. Separately, mix remaining ¼ cup sugar, cornstarch, egg yolks, salt, and remaining ¼ cup milk into a smooth batter. Whisk until lumps are gone.

4. Stir into boiled milk. Add raisins. Cook over low heat, stirring until thickened. Remove from heat.

5. Stir in sour cream, vanilla, and lemon juice. Cool.

6. Pour into baked pie shell and top with whipped cream.

To make a **Baked Pie Crust**, prepare crust from recipes on page 220. Preheat oven to 475°. Prick crust on sides and bottom with fork. Bake in preheated oven 8-10 minutes. Cool before filling.

German Chocolate Pie

½ cup unsweetened cocoa powder

4 cups sugar

3 Tbsp. all-purpose flour

½ cup (1 stick) butter, melted

6 eggs

12-oz. can evaporated milk, *or* 1½ cups heavy cream

2 tsp. vanilla

½ cup chopped pecans, *divided*

½ cup shredded coconut, *divided*

3 9" unbaked pie shells (see recipes on page 220)

1. Preheat oven to 350°.

2. Mix together cocoa powder, sugar, and flour in bowl. Add melted butter.

3. Beat in six eggs, one at a time.

4. Add evaporated milk or cream and vanilla.

5. Divide pecans and coconut evenly among pie shells.

6. Divide cocoa batter evenly among pie shells.

7. Bake in preheated oven 35–40 minutes, or until set. Cool and chill before serving.

Makes:

3 9" pies

Prep. Time:

20 minutes

Baking Time:

35–40 minutes

Chilling Time:

at least 2 hours

Tip:

Garnish with whipped cream before serving if desired.

A friend lamented that her neighbor cleaned the fencerow where she used to pick elderberries. I sympathized, because one of my favorite summer treats is picking wild berries. If every farmer had at least one overgrown fencerow, think of all who would benefit from it.

Never Fail Pie Crust

3 cups pastry flour
1 cup lard
1 tsp. salt

1 Tbsp. sugar, *optional*
1½ tsp. vinegar
scant ½ cup milk

Makes:

3 9" pie crusts, or
1 double crust and
1 single crust

Prep. Time:

25 minutes

1. In large bowl, mix together flour, lard, salt, and sugar if you wish with pastry blender.

2. Put vinegar in a one-half-cup measure. Fill one-half cup with milk. Let stand several minutes.

3. Add soured milk gradually to flour mixture, stirring in with a fork.

4. Work dough a bit with hands to make 3 smooth balls.

5. Roll out each ball with rolling pin on floured board.

6. Place each flattened crust into 9" pie pan.

This is my favorite crust recipe. It comes from my mother-in-law, and she was the one who got me into pie-baking. The sour milk makes a dough that does not become tough if you handle it too much.

Pie Crust

3 cups pastry flour
1 cup shortening
½ tsp. salt

1 egg
5 Tbsp. ice water
1 tsp. vinegar

Makes:

3 9" pie crusts, or
1 double crust and
1 single crust

Prep. Time:

25 minutes

1. Mix flour, shortening, and salt in a good-sized bowl.

2. Beat egg in separate bowl. Stir in water and vinegar.

3. Add liquid ingredients to flour mixture, a bit at a time—enough to make a soft dough.

4. Divide into 3 balls. Roll each out on floured board and place in 9" pie pan.

The "Farm Home" Cookbook

DESSERTS

Peach Cobbler

4 cups sliced peaches
½ cup (1 stick) butter, melted
1½ cups sugar, *divided*
3 tsp. vanilla
¾ tsp. salt
½ cup milk
1 tsp. baking powder
1 cup all-purpose flour
½ cup hot water

Makes:

6-8 servings

Prep. Time:

20 minutes

Baking Time:

1 hour

1. Preheat oven to 350°.

2. Place peaches in greased 9" × 13" baking pan.

3. In good-sized bowl, mix together butter, ½ cup sugar, vanilla, salt, milk, baking powder, and flour until smooth.

4. Pour over fruit in baking pan.

5. Mix remaining 1 cup sugar and hot water. Pour over batter. Do NOT stir.

6. Bake in preheated oven 1 hour. Eat warm with milk.

You may substitute apples or other fresh fruit.

Libby's Great Rhubarb Cobbler

4 cups rhubarb, cut into 1" pieces

1 cup + 1 Tbsp. sugar, *divided*

2 Tbsp. cornstarch *or* Clear Jel

3 Tbsp. water

1½ Tbsp. + ¼ cup (half stick) butter, *divided*

1 cup all-purpose flour

1½ tsp. baking powder

¼ tsp. salt

2 tsp. grated orange peel

¼ cup milk

1 egg

Makes:

6 servings

Prep. Time:

20 minutes

Baking Time:

40 minutes

1. Preheat oven to 400°.

2. In a saucepan, whisk together 1 cup sugar, cornstarch, and water. Stir in rhubarb.

3. Bring to boil, then continue to cook and stir mixture for 1 minute.

4. Pour into greased 8" round baking dish.

5. Dot with 1½ Tbsp. butter.

6. In mixing bowl, use a pastry cutter to cut ¼ cup butter into flour, remaining 1 Tbsp. sugar, baking powder, salt, and orange peel. Continue until mixture resembles coarse crumbs.

7. In separate bowl, mix milk and egg together. Add all at once to crumb mixture. Stir.

8. Drop by tablespoonful over rhubarb mixture.

9. Bake in preheated oven 40 minutes, or until crust is browned.

10. Serve with cream or vanilla ice cream.

Magic Cobbler

¼ cup (half stick) butter
1 cup sugar
1 cup all-purpose flour
1½ tsp. baking powder
¾ cup milk
3-4 cups fruit of your choice: sliced peaches, chopped apples,
   or berries, sugared lightly, according to taste

Makes:

6-8 servings

Prep. Time:

10 minutes

Baking Time:

30 minutes

1. Melt butter in 9" × 13" baking pan as oven preheats to 350°.

2. Meanwhile, mix sugar, flour, baking powder, and milk together.

3. Pour batter over melted butter. Do not stir.

4. Add fruit in an even layer. Sprinkle sugar over fruit if you wish.

5. Bake in preheated oven 30 minutes. Cake rises during baking.

6. Serve hot or cold with milk.

Growing up, and also with our own children, we'd sit in a circle—capping strawberries, shelling peas, shucking and cleaning corn, snapping beans, peeling peaches and pears— singing or playing word games as we worked. Anybody for "Initials" or another brain game?!

Fruit Platz

2¼ cups all-purpose flour, *divided*

1½ tsp. baking powder

¼ tsp. salt

½ cup (1 stick) + 1 Tbsp. butter, *divided*

½ cup milk

4 cups fruit, cut in large chunks: a mixture of peaches, plums, apricots, nectarines, sweet cherries, blueberries, etc.

½ –1 cup sugar, depending on the sweetness of the fruit

¾ cup brown sugar

1 tsp. cinnamon

½ tsp. nutmeg

Makes:

8-10 servings

Prep. Time:

20 minutes

Baking Time:

40 minutes

Tip:

This is best eaten on the day it's made.

1. Preheat oven to 375°.

2. In mixing bowl, combine 1½ cups flour, baking powder, and salt.

3. Using a pastry cutter or two knives, cut in ½ cup butter until crumbs form. Stir in milk.

4. Mix with fork until ball of soft dough forms.

5. Press into greased 9" × 13" baking pan.

6. Mix sugar and fruit. Spread over dough.

7. Mix brown sugar, remaining 1 Tbsp. butter, remaining ¾ cup flour, cinnamon, and nutmeg together until crumbly. Scatter over fruit.

8. Bake in preheated oven 35-45 minutes, until golden.

Very Berry Crunch

6 cups fresh berries—raspberries, blueberries, blackberries, boysenberries, etc.
1 Tbsp. + ¾ cup all-purpose flour, *divided*
¾ cup dry rolled oats
⅓ cup (5⅓ Tbsp.) butter, softened
⅔ cup brown sugar
⅓ cup chopped nuts

Makes:

8-10 servings

Prep. Time:

15 minutes

Baking Time:

30 minutes

1. Preheat oven to 375°.

2. Combine berries in a bowl. Dust lightly with 1 Tbsp. flour and gently mix.

3. Pour into a greased 9" × 9" baking pan.

4. In a bowl, mix ¾ cup flour, rolled oats, butter, brown sugar, and nuts together with hands until crumbly.

5. Sprinkle topping over fruit.

6. Bake in preheated oven about 30 minutes. Fruit should be bubbly and top golden brown.

7. Serve warm with ice cream, yogurt, or whipped cream.

Rhubarb Butter Crunch

3 cups diced rhubarb
1 cup sugar
3 Tbsp. + 1 ½ cups all-
purpose flour, *divided*

1 cup brown sugar
1 cup dry rolled oats
½ cup (1 stick) butter, cut in
chunks

Makes:

6-8 servings

Prep. Time:

15 minutes

Baking Time:

40 minutes

1. Preheat oven to 375°.

2. Combine rhubarb, sugar, and 3 Tbsp. flour in bowl. Place in greased 8" × 8" baking dish or equivalent.

3. In same bowl, combine brown sugar, oats, and 1½ cups flour.

4. Using a pastry cutter or two knives, cut in butter until pea-sized crumbs form. Sprinkle over rhubarb mixture.

5. Bake in preheated oven 40 minutes, until bubbly and top is browned. Serve with milk.

Pumpkin Crunch

3 cups cooked, pureed pumpkin
   (plain canned pumpkin is fine)
2½ cups milk
3 Tbsp. all-purpose flour
6 eggs
1 cup sugar
1 cup brown sugar
½ tsp. salt
1 tsp. cinnamon
½ tsp. nutmeg
½ tsp. allspice

Crunch Topping
2 cups all-purpose flour
1 tsp. baking soda
2 cups dry rolled oats
¼ tsp. salt
⅔ cup brown sugar
¾ cup (1½ sticks) butter

Makes:

12-15 servings

Prep. Time:

25 minutes

Baking Time:

55 minutes

1. Preheat oven to 400°.

2. Make filling by mixing pumpkin, milk, flour, eggs, sugar, brown sugar, salt, cinnamon, nutmeg, and allspice together in good-sized bowl. Beat well with wire whisk or egg beater.

3. Pour into greased 9" × 13" baking pan.

4. Make crunch topping by combining flour, baking soda, oats, salt, and brown sugar. Using a pastry cutter or two knives, cut in butter until pea-sized crumbs form.

5. Sprinkle crumb mixture over top of pumpkin mixture.

6. Bake in preheated oven 10 minutes. Lower heat to 350° and bake 40-45 more minutes, or until a knife inserted into filling 1" from side of baking pan comes out clean. The center may still look soft but will set later as it cools.

Raspberry Crunch

3 cups fresh raspberries

1¾ cups sugar, *divided*

½ cup chopped pecans

2 eggs

½ cup (1 stick) butter, melted

1 cup all-purpose flour

Makes:

6–8 servings

Prep. Time:

15 minutes

Baking Time:

1 hour

1. Preheat oven to 325°.

2. Place fruit in greased 8" × 8" baking dish.

3. Sprinkle with ¾ cup sugar and ½ cup pecans.

4. In mixing bowl, beat eggs, butter, flour, and remaining 1 cup sugar until smooth.

5. Spread over fruit mixture.

6. Bake in preheated oven 1 hour or until toothpick comes out clean. Serve with ice cream.

A gathering walk into the garden often yields an entire meal. We do successive plantings so we can keep fresh vegetables on the table all summer and fall, saving the food on the canning shelves for winter.

Applesauce Bread Pudding

8 slices bread, stale *or* lightly toasted, *divided*
2½ cups applesauce, *divided*
⅓ cup raisins
¾ cup brown sugar, *divided*
½ tsp. cinnamon
2 eggs
2 cups milk
½ tsp. vanilla
¼ tsp. salt
dash nutmeg

Makes:

6-8 servings

Prep. Time:

20 minutes

Baking Time:

55-60 minutes

1. Preheat oven to 350°.

2. Arrange 4 slices bread in bottom of greased 9" × 9" baking pan.

3. In bowl, combine 2 cups applesauce, raisins, ¼ cup brown sugar, and cinnamon.

4. Spread over bread. Then top with 4 remaining pieces of bread.

5. In bowl, beat together eggs, milk, vanilla, remaining ½ cup brown sugar, salt, and nutmeg.

6. Pour mixture over bread. Spread final ½ cup applesauce gently over bread.

7. Bake in preheated oven 55-60 minutes. Serve warm or cold.

Rich Strawberry Shortcakes

2 cups all-purpose flour
2 Tbsp. sugar
4 tsp. baking powder
½ tsp. salt
½ cup (1 stick) butter, softened
1 egg
½ cup light cream *or* milk
soft butter
6 cups sweetened sliced *or* chopped strawberries
whipped cream, milk, *or* ice cream

Makes:

4 servings

Prep. Time:

10 minutes

Baking Time:

8 minutes

Variation:

These shortcakes are good with any fruit in season.

1. Preheat oven to 450°.

2. Mix together flour, sugar, baking powder, and salt in good-sized bowl. Using a pastry cutter or two knives, cut in butter till pea-sized crumbs form.

3. In a separate bowl, combine egg and cream. Add to flour mixture, stirring just until dough follows fork around bowl.

4. On lightly floured surface, roll dough out to ½" thickness. Cut with 2½" round cutter.

5. Bake shortcakes on ungreased baking sheets in preheated oven about 8 minutes.

6. Split biscuits, spread with butter, and spoon berries over them. Serve warm with whipped cream, milk, or ice cream.

This is often a supper dish for us during strawberry season. We don't bother splitting the shortcakes in half but just break them in pieces, and then add strawberries and milk. Swiss cheese goes well on the side.

Strawberry Tapioca Pudding

4 cups water
½ cup + 1 Tbsp. baby pearl tapioca
3-oz. pkg. strawberry gelatin
⅔ cup sugar
1½ cups heavy cream
3-4 bananas, sliced
2 cups halved strawberries

Makes:

8-10 servings

Prep. Time:

15 minutes

Cooking Time:

10 minutes

Cooling/Standing
Time:

1½ hours

1. Bring water to boil in saucepan. Stir in tapioca. Cover. Turn off heat and let stand until tapioca is clear, about 15 minutes.

2. Reheat tapioca until hot and steaming. Stir in powdered gelatin and sugar.

3. Uncover and cool.

4. When completely cool, whip cream in separate bowl.

5. Fold whipped cream into tapioca. Fold in bananas and strawberries.

It's strawberry season, and tonight's supper is a favorite during this time of year. Hot biscuits just out of the oven, crumbled into soup bowls, covered with fresh crushed strawberries, and then just the right amount of cold milk.

Honeyed Fruit

1 pint strawberries
1 pint blueberries
½ cup honey

1. Wash and drain fruit. Slice strawberries if you wish.

2. Toss berries lightly with honey.

3. Serve with pound cake, ice cream, or vanilla pudding for a simple dessert.

Makes:

6–8 servings

Prep. Time:

10 minutes

Fresh Peach and Berry Melba

4 ripe peaches
½ cup raspberries
½ cup blueberries
2 tsp. honey
½ tsp. orange zest
4 scoops French vanilla *or* peach ice cream, *divided*
1 cup whipped cream, *divided*
2 Tbsp. slivered almonds

Makes:

4 servings

Prep. Time:

10 minutes

Cooking Time:

5-10 minutes

1. Peel and slice peaches into 4 dessert bowls.

2. To make sauce, combine berries, honey, and zest in small saucepan.

3. Cook over low heat, mashing berries with fork until combined, warm, and spongy.

4. Top each peach with a scoop of ice cream.

5. Pour warm sauce over, top with ¼ cup whipped cream, and sprinkle with almonds. Serve immediately.

Stewed Sweet Apples

3 cups sliced sweet apples
2 cups water
⅔ cup brown sugar
¼ tsp. salt
4 tsp. all-purpose flour
½ cup milk *or* cream
cinnamon

Makes:

4-6 servings

Prep. Time:

10 minutes

1. Peel and core apples. Then cut in thin slices lengthwise.

2. In a medium saucepan, combine apples and water. Bring to a simmer and cook 3 minutes. Apples should be crisp-tender.

3. Stir in sugar and salt.

4. Add milk to flour in small bowl. Whisk to a smooth paste.

5. Gently stir paste into apples, continuing to stir over low to medium heat until slightly thickened.

6. Remove from heat, pour into serving dish, and cool. Sprinkle with cinnamon just before serving.

Cooking Time:

15 minutes

Cooling Time:

at least 30 minutes

Chocolate Praline Ice Cream Topping

1 cup heavy cream
⅔ cup brown sugar, packed
⅔ cup (1 stick + 2⅔ Tbsp.) butter
1 cup chocolate chips
1 cup chopped pecans

Makes:

3 cups

Cooking Time:

8-10 minutes

1. In a saucepan over medium heat, bring cream, brown sugar, and butter to a boil, stirring constantly.

2. Reduce heat. Simmer 2 minutes, stirring occasionally.

3. Remove from heat. Stir in chocolate chips until melted and smooth.

4. Stir in pecans. Serve warm over ice cream.

5. Store in refrigerator.

Frozen Cheesecake

8 whole graham crackers, crushed

3 Tbsp. + 1 cup sugar, *divided*

¼ cup (half stick) butter, melted

1 cup heavy cream

2 8-oz. pkgs. cream cheese,
softened (see recipe on page 273)

4 eggs*

1 tsp. vanilla

fruit, for serving

* If you prefer, skip raw eggs and use pasteurized eggs.

Makes:

15 servings

Prep. Time:

25 minutes

Freezing Time:

2–3 hours

Standing Time:

20–30 minutes

1. Combine crushed crackers, 3 Tbsp. sugar, and butter in mixing bowl.

2. Press into 9" × 13" pan to form crust. Cover and place in freezer.

3. Make filling by beating heavy cream until it becomes 2 cups whipped cream.

4. In another bowl, beat cream cheese with 1 cup sugar. Beat in vanilla and eggs.

5. Fold in whipped cream. Spoon over top of graham cracker crust.

6. Cover. Freeze 2-3 hours before serving.

7. Set out cheesecake 20-30 minutes before you want to serve it. Serve topped with your choice of fruit.

Our Favorite Ice Cream

1½ Tbsp. plain gelatin
¼ cup cold water
7 cups milk
2½ cups maple syrup

3 eggs
6 Tbsp. cornstarch
heavy cream

Makes:

Fills a 1½ gallon ice cream freezer

Prep. Time:

20 minutes

Cooking Time:

15 minutes

Chilling Time:

2 hours or more

1. In small bowl, whisk together gelatin and water. Set aside to soften for 5 minutes.

2. In a saucepan, heat milk and maple syrup together until scalding.

3. In separate bowl, beat eggs. Add cornstarch. Beat again.

4. Stir into hot milk–maple syrup mixture, stirring until thickened.

5. Cool pudding and chill until cold, 2 hours or more.

6. Pour cold pudding into 1½ gallon ice cream freezer. Add enough cream so that freezer is filled to within 4 inches of the top. Freeze and enjoy.

Lizzie Pudding

1 cup graham cracker crumbs
1 Tbsp. brown sugar
¼ cup (half stick) butter, melted
¾ cup heavy cream
6 oz. cream cheese, softened (see recipe on page 273)
6 Tbsp. confectioners sugar
¾ tsp. vanilla
4 cups pie filling of your choice

Makes:

10–12 servings

Prep. Time:

20 minutes

Chilling Time:

at least 3 hours

1. In a bowl, mix graham cracker crumbs, brown sugar, and butter together.

2. Press into greased 9" × 9" baking pan.

3. Whip the cream. Cut cream cheese into chunks. Add to whipped cream and beat together.

4. Add confectioners sugar and vanilla. Beat together well.

5. Spread filling over graham cracker crust. Cover and refrigerate for at least 3 hours.

6. Top with pie filling of your choice. Serve chilled.

This type of dessert was introduced back in the '60s and called "cream cheese dessert." When our children were young, someone named Lizzie brought this dessert to a reunion and the name was picked up and stuck. It's easier to say and has more color than the original, wouldn't you agree?!

The "Farm Home" Cookbook

APPETIZERS, SNACKS, and BEVERAGES

Italian Stuffed Appetizer Bread

1 lb. bulk sausage of your choice
½ cup sliced red bell pepper
1 lb. bread dough
4 oz. cream cheese, softened (see recipe on page 273)
2 garlic cloves, minced
⅓ cup pitted, sliced olives
2 cups shredded Swiss cheese
1–2 Tbsp. water
1 tsp. poppy seeds

Makes:

10 servings

Prep. Time:

20 minutes

Baking Time:

20–25 minutes

Standing Time:

10 minutes

1. Brown sausage in skillet. Remove sausage from skillet, leaving drippings behind.

2. Sauté red peppers in drippings in same skillet.

3. On lightly floured surface, roll bread dough to a 16" × 12" rectangle.

4. Combine cream cheese and garlic. Spread lengthwise over center third of dough.

5. Top with sausage, peppers, olives, and Swiss cheese.

6. Preheat oven to 400°.

7. Fold one lengthwise side of dough over filling. Brush lightly with water along an inch or two of the edge.

8. Fold other lengthwise side of dough over filling, overlapping onto wet edge. Pinch together to make a tight seal.

9. With sharp knife, make slits down the middle every 2" to expose filling.

10. Brush lightly with water and sprinkle with poppy seeds.

11. Bake in preheated oven 20–25 minutes or until golden brown.

12. Let stand 10 minutes before slicing.

Garden Cheese Pinwheels

8 10" flour tortillas

4 oz. cream cheese, room temperature (see recipe on page 273)

1 lb. thinly sliced cooked turkey

1 cup shredded carrots, *divided*

1 cup shredded lettuce, *divided*

2 cups shredded cheese, *divided*

seasonings such as garlic salt *or* seasoning salt, pepper, and fresh
    chopped parsley

(see recipe on page 273)

1. Spread cream cheese evenly over each tortilla, covering to the edge.

2. Top each tortilla with turkey slices, 2 Tbsp. carrots, 2 Tbsp. lettuce, and ¼ cup cheese, leaving a ½" border around the edge.

3. Add any seasonings desired. Roll up fairly tightly.

4. Wrap securely in plastic wrap and refrigerate for at least one hour.

5. Slice into ½" slices for pinwheels and serve on platter.

Makes:

8–10 servings

Prep. Time:

15 minutes

Chilling Time:

at least 1 hour

Variations:

We sometimes eat these as wraps instead of cutting them in slices. No need to refrigerate first in that case.

Besides being good appetizers, these roll-ups are also good for a light supper around the picnic table on a warm summer evening when it's too warm to cook. Add some potato chips and milk shakes with good Jersey milk, fresh fruit, and yogurt.

Use half cream cheese and half mayonnaise to spread on tortillas.

Soft Pretzels

1¾ cups lukewarm water,
  divided
2 Tbsp. yeast
4½ cups all-purpose flour
1¼ tsp. salt

2 tsp. baking soda
melted butter, for brushing
coarse pretzel salt *or*
  cinnamon sugar, for
  sprinkling

Makes:

8-10 servings

Prep. Time:

30 minutes

Baking Time:

15 minutes

Variation:

Instead of making into pretzel shapes, we like to roll the dough out and cut into strips 4-6" long. After brushing with melted butter, we sprinkle them with garlic salt and Parmesan cheese. Then dip them in pizza sauce before taking a bite. Delicious!

1. In a mixing bowl, dissolve yeast in 1½ cups lukewarm water.

2. Stir in flour and salt. Knead well.

3. Divide dough into lumps (any size, as long as they're equal).

4. Roll lumps into snakes with hands. Form into pretzel shapes.

5. Preheat oven to 400°.

6. Mix remaining ¼ cup water with baking soda in shallow bowl.

7. Dip each pretzel in baking soda solution.

8. Lay on greased baking sheets.

9. Bake in preheated oven 15 minutes.

10. Brush hot pretzels with melted butter as soon as you've taken them out of the oven.

11. Immediately sprinkle with coarse pretzel salt or cinnamon sugar.

12. Dip into pizza sauce, strawberry jam, cheese sauce— the choice is yours!

Soft pretzels are a good family project. And we have friends who once a year invite guests to come for soft pretzels and something to drink. They make pretzels all evening long until everyone has had all they want.

Corn Chips

1 cup yellow cornmeal
½ cup all-purpose flour
1 tsp. salt
1 tsp. baking powder
½ cup milk
¼ cup (half stick) melted butter

½ tsp. Worcestershire sauce
¼ tsp. hot sauce
paprika
garlic, onion, *or* seasoning
   salt

Makes:

4-6 servings

Prep. Time:

20 minutes

Baking Time:

10 minutes

1. In a mixing bowl, combine cornmeal, flour, salt, and baking powder.

2. In a separate bowl, combine milk, butter, Worcestershire sauce, and hot sauce.

3. Add liquids to cornmeal mixture. Stir with fork. Knead a little until smooth.

4. Grease two baking sheets and sprinkle with cornmeal.

5. Preheat oven to 350°.

6. Divide dough in half. With floured rolling pin, roll out each half directly onto baking sheet, rolling dime-thin.

7. Sprinkle lightly with paprika and garlic, onion, or seasoning salt. Run rolling pin over once more to press in seasoning.

8. Prick dough with fork. Cut into squares or triangles.

9. Bake in preheated oven 10 minutes, or until lightly browned.

10. Cool and store in an airtight container.

Wheat Thins

2 cups whole wheat flour
2 Tbsp. wheat germ
1 tsp. salt
1 tsp. baking powder
2 Tbsp. brown sugar
2 Tbsp. dry milk powder
6 Tbsp. (¾ stick) butter, room temperature
½ cup water
1 Tbsp. mild molasses
cornmeal
paprika
garlic, onion, *or* seasoning salt

Makes

3 cups crackers

Prep. Time:

20 minutes

Baking Time:

10-12 minutes

1. In mixing bowl, combine flour, wheat germ, salt, baking powder, brown sugar, and dry milk.

2. Cut in butter with pastry blender.

3. In a separate bowl, combine water and molasses. Stir into flour mixture.

4. Knead a little until smooth.

5. Grease two baking sheets and sprinkle with cornmeal.

6. Preheat oven to 350°.

7. Divide dough in half.

8. Roll out each half of dough directly onto baking sheet with floured rolling pin, dime-thin.

9. Sprinkle lightly with paprika and your choice of garlic, onion, or seasoning salt.

10. Run rolling pin over once more to press seasonings into dough.

11. Prick with fork. Cut in squares or triangles.

12. Bake 10 minutes in preheated oven or until lightly browned.

13. Cool and store in an airtight container.

Ritz Crackers

2 cups whole wheat flour
1 Tbsp. baking powder
1 tsp. salt, *divided*
1 Tbsp. sugar
½ cup (1 stick) butter, *divided*, plus more for brushing
½ cup water

1. In bowl, mix together flour, baking powder, ½ tsp. salt, and sugar.

2. Cut in 6 Tbsp. (¾ stick) cold butter with pastry blender.

3. In a separate bowl, mix together water and remaining 2 Tbsp. butter, melted. Set aside.

4. Preheat oven to 350°.

5. Roll dough out dime-thin onto greased and liberally floured baking sheet, adding flour as needed.

6. Prick dough with fork. Cut into crackers.

7. Bake in preheated oven until golden, about 10 minutes.

8. Cool 10 minutes and then rotate crackers—putting ones in center out to edges.

9. Reduce oven temperature to 300°.

10. Brush crackers with melted butter and water mixture.

11. Sprinkle with remaining ½ tsp. salt.

12. Bake 30 minutes in preheated oven.

13. Cool and store in an airtight container.

Makes:

about 2 cups

Prep. Time:

15 minutes

Baking Time:

40 minutes

Variation:

May use garlic salt or other flavored salt for the second baking – whatever flavor you like.

Crispy Caramel Corn

7 quarts popped corn, unpopped kernels removed
2 cups brown sugar
½ cup light corn syrup
1 cup (2 sticks) butter
1 tsp. salt
½ tsp. baking soda
1 tsp. vanilla

Makes:

8 quarts

Prep. Time:

15 minutes

Cooking/Baking Time:

1 hour 10 minutes

1. Place popcorn in large bowl.

2. Place brown sugar, corn syrup, butter, and salt in large saucepan.

3. Bring to a boil, uncovered, and boil five minutes.

4. Preheat oven to 250°.

5. Remove syrup from stove. Stir in baking soda and vanilla.

6. Immediately pour over popcorn and mix quickly and well.

7. Pour onto lightly greased rimmed baking sheets or large baking pans.

8. Bake in preheated oven one hour. Stir several times during baking.

9. Serve immediately or store in airtight container.

Apfel Kuchen (Apple Fritters)

1¼ cups all-purpose flour
2 tsp. baking powder
¼ tsp. salt
2 eggs
⅔ cups milk

2 cups peeled, diced apples,
    about 3 apples
coconut oil
sugar, for rolling

Makes:

15–18 fritters

Prep. Time:

20 minutes

Cooking Time:

20 minutes

1. In a mixing bowl, blend dry ingredients together.

2. In a separate bowl, beat eggs and add milk.

3. Pour wet ingredients into flour mixture, stirring until smooth.

4. Stir apples into batter.

5. Heat 1" coconut oil in heavy pan to 375°.

6. Drop batter by the tablespoon into hot oil. Cook until golden on one side. Turn and repeat on other side.

7. Drain fritters on paper towels. Roll in sugar while warm.

Summer is such a busy time, it's easy to forget to take time for small pleasures. Take your children or grandchildren on picnics, go wading in the creek, take them along berry picking, make grape-juice popsicles!

Pepper Poppers

8 oz. cream cheese, softened
(see recipe on page 273)

1 cup shredded cheddar cheese

1 cup shredded Monterey Jack
cheese

⅓ cup fried bacon pieces
(about 6 slices)

¼ tsp. salt

¼ tsp. chili powder

¼ tsp. garlic powder

1 lb. fresh jalapenos, halved
lengthwise and seeded

½ cup dry bread crumbs

1. Combine three cheeses, bacon, salt, chili powder, and garlic powder in bowl. Mix well.

2. Preheat oven to 300°.

3. Spoon about 2 Tbsp. mixture into each pepper half.

4. Roll filled pepper halves in bread crumbs.

5. Place on greased baking sheet.

6. Bake uncovered in preheated oven 20 minutes. The longer they bake, the milder they get, so bake them according to your preference.

Makes:

about 24

Prep. Time:

25 minutes

Baking Time:

20 minutes

Tip:

When cutting and seeding hot peppers, wear plastic gloves to protect your hands.

Mozzarella Sticks

1-lb. block mozzarella cheese
½ cup all-purpose flour
2 eggs
2 Tbsp. water
1½ cups plain, dry bread crumbs

½ tsp. seasoning salt
¼ tsp. garlic powder
coconut oil
favorite pizza sauce, for
   dipping

Makes:

10 servings

Prep. Time:

25 minutes

Chilling Time:

1 hour

Cooking Time:

5-10 minutes

1. Cut cheese into 32 sticks.

2. In a bag, shake cheese sticks with flour until well coated.

3. In shallow bowl, beat eggs with water.

4. In another bowl, combine bread crumbs, seasoning salt, and garlic powder.

5. Dip floured cheese sticks, one at a time, in egg mixture.

6. Then roll in crumb mixture until well coated.

7. Place on large baking sheet and chill one hour (or longer).

8. Heat 1½" coconut oil in heavy saucepan to 370°.

9. Fry sticks, 3 or 4 at a time, for about 3 to 5 *seconds* until golden brown. Watch closely — it goes fast!

10. Remove with slotted spoon and drain on paper towels.

11. Serve with your favorite pizza sauce for dipping. These are also good with soup.

Goat Cheese Spreads

6 oz. soft goat cheese
salt and pepper, to taste
toasted baguette slices *or* crackers, for serving

Combine with (pick one):

a:

¼ cup pesto

b:

3 tsp. chopped
oil-packed dried
tomatoes
1 tsp. minced fresh
thyme

c:

¼ cup toasted
pistachios
2 tsp. finely chopped
fresh chives

Makes:

6 servings

Prep. Time:

10 minutes

1. In a bowl, mash goat cheese with fork. Season with salt and pepper.

2. Mix gently with option a, b, or c.

3. Serve with toasted baguette slices or your favorite crackers.

Green Dip

1 cup steamed kale, chard, *or*
spinach, liquid squeezed out
and discarded
1 cup cooked chickpeas
¾ cup plain yogurt
⅓ cup mayonnaise (see recipe
on page 65)

2 cloves garlic
5 scallions, chopped
1 Tbsp. lemon juice
½ tsp. salt, *or* to taste
¼ tsp. dry mustard
fresh veggies *or* crackers,
for serving

Makes:

2½ cups

Prep. Time:

10 minutes

1. Puree all ingredients in blender or food processor.

2. Chill.

3. Serve with fresh veggies or crackers.

Radish Dip

8 oz. cream cheese, softened
 (see recipe on page 273)
½ cup sour cream
2 cups chopped radishes
1 Tbsp. chopped chives

2 Tbsp. minced onion
½ tsp. seasoning salt, *or* to
 taste
⅛ tsp. pepper
chips *or* crackers, for serving

Makes:

3 cups

Prep. Time:

10 minutes

1. In bowl, whip cream cheese until softened. Fold sour cream into whipped cheese.

2. Stir in remaining ingredients.

3. Serve with chips or crackers.

Taco Dip

8 oz. cream cheese, at room
    temperature (see recipe on
    page 273)
¼ cup sugar *or* honey
1 cup sour cream
¾ cup salad dressing (see
    recipe on page 64)
1 lb. ground beef
1 cup salsa

1½ Tbsp. taco seasoning
    (see recipe on page 271)
shredded lettuce
chopped tomatoes
chopped onion
chopped green and red bell
    peppers
shredded cheese
tortilla chips, for serving

Makes:

10-15 servings

Prep. Time:

20 minutes

Chilling Time:

2 hours

1. In a bowl, mix softened cream cheese with sugar.

2. Stir in sour cream and salad dressing. Refrigerate 2 hours.

3. Meanwhile, brown ground beef with taco seasoning, then add salsa. Cool.

4. To assemble: spread cream cheese mixture on serving platter, top with beef mixture, then add other toppings in layers. Serve with tortilla chips.

Herb Garlic Spread

2 8-oz. pkgs. cream cheese,
    room temperature (see
    recipe on page 273)
¼ cup (half stick) butter,
    room temperature
½ tsp. dried basil
½ tsp. dried oregano
½ tsp. dried thyme

½ tsp. dried marjoram
½ tsp. dill weed
½ tsp. garlic powder
½ tsp. freshly ground black
    pepper
1 cup shredded cheese of
    your choice
crackers, for serving

Makes:

2 cups

Prep. Time:

15 minutes

Variation:

To use fresh
chopped herbs,
triple the amount.

1. Mix everything together well.

2. Spread on crackers and enjoy!

Real Onion Dip

1 Tbsp. butter
1 large onion, minced
1 cup cottage cheese

1 tsp. lemon juice
½ tsp. salt, *or* to taste
chives *or* parsley, to taste

Makes:

1½ cups

Prep. Time:

10 minutes

Cooking Time:

20–30 minutes

Variation:

For a richer dip, substitute Greek yogurt or sour cream for all or part of cottage cheese.

1. In skillet, melt butter. Add onion. Sauté over low heat until onion browns and caramelizes, 20 minutes or longer.

2. In food processor, puree cottage cheese. Add caramelized onions.

3. Add ¼ cup water to hot drippings in skillet where onion browned. Scrape well to get all the flavor and lift the browned bits. Add to food processor.

4. Add lemon juice, salt, and chives or parsley to processer.

5. Process until smooth. Taste for salt. Add up to ¼ cup more water if needed to reach the consistency you want.

Use as a salad dressing by making it pourable. Otherwise, this is great as a topping on baked potatoes or as a dip for fresh vegetables.

Creamy Spinach Dip

1 cup sour cream
1 cup mayonnaise (see recipe on page 65)
½ tsp. celery salt
½ tsp. dill weed
¼ tsp. onion powder
¼ cup chopped scallions
1½ cups torn fresh spinach
8 oz. water chestnuts, drained and finely chopped
fresh veggies *or* bread cubes, for serving

Makes

3 cups

Prep. Time:

15 minutes

Chilling Time:

1 hour minimum

1. In mixing bowl, combine sour cream, mayo, and seasonings.

2. Stir in scallions, spinach, and water chestnuts.

3. Cover and chill for at least an hour.

4. Serve as dip with veggies or bread cubes.

We love this dip in a bread bowl. Choose a large round loaf. Cut the middle core out to make a bowl. Cut up the bread core into chunks. Put the chilled dip in the bread bowl, and use the bread chunks as dippers. Don't forget to eat the bowl, too!

Warm Pizza Dip

8-oz. pkg. cream cheese, at room temperature (see recipe on page 273)

½ cup sour cream

1 tsp. dried oregano

cayenne pepper, a dash, *or* to taste

1 chopped garlic clove, *or* to taste

½ cup chopped pepperoni

½ cup chopped green bell pepper

½ cup chopped onion

½ cup pizza sauce

1 cup shredded cheese of your choice

crackers *or* Italian bread slices, for serving

Makes:

10-15 servings

Prep. Time:

15 minutes

Baking Time:

15 minutes

1. Preheat oven to 350°.

2. In a bowl, mix together cream cheese, sour cream, oregano, cayenne pepper, and garlic.

3. Spread on bottom of 9" × 9" baking pan.

4. Layer on pepperoni, green pepper, onion, and pizza sauce.

5. Bake in preheated oven 10 minutes. Sprinkle with cheese and bake 5 more minutes.

6. Serve with crackers or small slices of Italian bread.

Substitute ham cubes or bacon bits for pepperoni.

Caramel Dip

¼ cup (half stick) butter
1 cup brown sugar
8 oz. cream cheese (see recipe on page 273)
1 tsp. vanilla
1 cup sour cream
⅔ cup heavy cream
fresh fruit slices *or* crackers, for serving

Makes:

3 cups

Prep. Time:

10 minutes

Cooling/Chilling Time:

2–3 hours

1. In small saucepan, melt butter, brown sugar, and cream cheese together. Stir until well blended.

2. Remove from heat. Stir in vanilla.

3. Cool. Stir in sour cream.

4. Chill for at least 2 hours.

5. Whip cream in chilled bowl. Fold into chilled dip.

6. This is good served with apple slices or other fruit, but can also be used with crackers.

Lemon Verbena Dip

8 oz. cream cheese, at room temperature (see recipe on page 273)
8 oz. sour cream
2-3 Tbsp. chopped fresh lemon verbena leaves
¼ cup sugar
¼ cup fresh lemon juice
sliced apples *or* vanilla wafer cookies, for serving

1. Mix everything together in bowl.

2. Refrigerate several hours.

3. Serve with sliced apples or vanilla wafer cookies.

Makes:

2 cups

Prep. Time:

10 minutes

Chilling Time:

2-4 hours

Nippy Orange Dip

1 cup orange marmalade
1 Tbsp. prepared horseradish
½ tsp. black pepper
8 oz. cream cheese (see recipe on page 273)
crackers, for serving

Makes:

10–12 servings

Prep. Time:

10 minutes

1. In small bowl, combine marmalade, horseradish, and black pepper.

2. Place block of cream cheese of serving plate. Pour marmalade mixture over top.

3. Serve with crackers.

Lemon-Mint Quencher

5 cups water, *divided*
10 fresh mint leaves, plus mint sprigs for garnish
⅔ cup honey
1 tsp. grated lemon peel
1 cup lemon juice

Makes:

1½ quarts

Prep. Time:

10 minutes

Chilling Time:

at least 2 hours

1. In blender combine 1 cup water and mint leaves. Cover blender and process 1 minute.

2. Strain and discard chopped mint.

3. Pour minty water into pitcher.

4. Add rest of ingredients, including remaining 4 cups water. Stir until blended.

5. Cover and refrigerate for at least 2 hours. Serve over ice with mint sprigs as garnish.

Orange Minty

¾ cup fresh mint leaves,
 packed
3 cups water

⅓ cup sugar
2 cups orange juice
⅓ cup lemon juice

1. Put water and mint leaves in saucepan. Bring to boil, covered.

2. Turn off heat. Allow to steep, covered, for 30 minutes.

3. Strain out mint leaves and discard.

4. Add sugar and stir until dissolved. Set aside to cool.

5. In half-gallon serving pitcher, stir juices together.

6. Add mint tea.

7. Add water and ice to fill pitcher. Give a final stir and serve.

Makes:

a half-gallon

Prep. Time:

15 minutes

Steeping Time:

30 minutes

Cooling Time:

1 hour or so

Cooking Time:

5 minutes

Peachy Smoothie

2 cups peeled, chopped peaches
1½ cups vanilla yogurt (see recipe
 on page 272)
1 cup milk
2 Tbsp. honey *or* sugar, to taste

*Try using
other fruits too.*

1. Puree peaches in blender.

2. Add rest of ingredients. Puree until smooth.

3. Pour into glasses and serve.

Makes:

2-3 servings

Prep. Time:

10 minutes

Variation:

For a thinner
smoothie, replace
yogurt with milk.

Mint Tea Concentrate

4 cups water
6 cups mint leaves, tightly packed
1½ cups sugar

1. Boil water in saucepan. Submerge mint leaves fully in hot water.

2. Let steep for 15 minutes with pan covered.

3. Add 1½ cups sugar. Stir until dissolved.

4. When concentrate cools, put in containers to freeze.

5. To serve, use 3 parts water to 1 part tea concentrate.

Makes:

5 cups concentrate

Prep. Time:

10 minutes

Cooking Time:

20 minutes

Steeping Time:

15 minutes

Fruit Smoothies

2 cups plain yogurt

¼ cup blueberries

1 cup chopped strawberries

1 cup frozen peaches

1 frozen banana

¼ cup sugar *or* honey

½ cup pineapple juice

1 Tbsp. lemon juice

Makes:

2–4 servings

Prep. Time:

5 minutes

Mix all ingredients in blender until smooth.

It's best if some of the fruit is frozen.
But if you're using all fresh fruit,
not frozen, add some ice cubes.

Strawberry Milkshake

1½ cups chopped strawberries
4 cups milk
1 pint (2 cups) strawberry ice cream

Makes:

4 servings

Prep. Time:

5 minutes

1. Combine all ingredients in blender at high speed for about 1 minute.

2. Pour into glasses and serve.

Pumpkin Eggnog

1 cup cooked, mashed pumpkin
10 fresh organic eggs*
½ tsp. salt
1½ cups sugar *or* maple syrup
1 tsp. vanilla
1 tsp. ground nutmeg
milk, as needed

* If you prefer, skip the raw eggs and use pasteurized eggs.

Makes:

1 gallon

Prep. Time:

10 minutes

1. Place pumpkin, eggs, salt, sugar, vanilla, nutmeg, and vanilla in blender. Blend until well mixed. (Vigorous beating with a rotary beater works well, too.)

2. Pour into a one-gallon pitcher and add enough milk to make one gallon. Stir to mix the added milk, then serve. (If you wish, add more milk to thin the eggnog.)

Hot Chocolate

2 squares unsweetened chocolate
⅛ tsp. salt
⅓ cup sugar
½ cup hot water
4 cups milk
whipped cream, *or* marshmallows, for serving

Makes:

6 servings

Prep. Time:

5 minutes

Cooking Time:

12–15 minutes

1. Get boiling water going in the bottom of a double boiler. Grate chocolate in top of double boiler. Place top over boiling water.

2. Add salt, sugar, salt, and ½ cup hot water to grated chocolate. Stir until a smooth paste forms.

3. Place chocolate mixture into saucepan over direct heat. Cook syrup 3 minutes.

4. Stir in milk gradually. Heat to boiling point.

5. Beat until frothy. Pour into mugs.

6. Add whipped cream or marshmallows to each cup.

Variation:

Make Hot Chocolate using chocolate syrup (page 268) instead. Use 2 Tbsp. syrup per cup of milk. Then follow Steps 4 through 6.

Pumpkin Latte

1 cup milk
½ cup strong brewed coffee
¼ tsp. cinnamon *or* pumpkin pie spice
½ tsp. vanilla
2 Tbsp. pumpkin puree
1 Tbsp. maple syrup
5 drops stevia, *or* sweetener of choice

Makes:

1 Serving

Prep. Time:

5 minutes

Cooking Time:

5 minutes

1. Put all ingredients in saucepan or microwave. Heat and stir.

2. Pour into your favorite mug and enjoy.

Chocolate Syrup

1½ cups sugar
pinch salt
1 tsp. cornstarch
½ cup unsweetened cocoa powder
1 cup hot water, *divided*
2 tsp. vanilla

1. Mix sugar, salt, cornstarch, and cocoa powder together in saucepan.

2. Whisk in enough water to make a paste. When smooth, add remaining water.

3. Bring to a boil, stirring constantly. Boil 3 minutes.

4. Add vanilla. Pour into a jar at once. Cap with lid. When cool, place in refrigerator.

Makes

2 cups

Prep. Time:

10 minutes

Cooking Time:

10 minutes

Cooling Time:

1-2 hours

Good for making chocolate milk or as a topping for ice cream.

Cake Flour

1. If you don't have cake flour, put 2 Tbsp. cornstarch in a one-cup measure.

2. Then fill it up with unsifted all-purpose flour.

3. Sift the mixture together three times.

4. One cup of this is equal to 1 cup sifted cake flour. It works very well for angel food cakes.

Italian Herb Seasonings

dried oregano
dried rosemary
dried basil

dried thyme
dried marjoram

1. Place equal amounts in a blender and whirl just until blended.

2. Store in a covered jar or bottle.

3. Use to enhance pasta sauces, tomato recipes, salad dressings, and cooked vegetables.

4. Rub dried herbs between your fingers before adding them to recipes. This releases natural oils, the source of their flavors.

During my growing up years, we picked bushels of elderberries every summer and sold them to Smucker's, who had a pick-up place at a local store. This was our spending money (to spend wisely!), which greatly aided our ambition. Mom also made a lot of elderberry jelly for our family's use.

Taco Seasoning

6 tsp. chili powder
4½ tsp. ground cumin
2½ tsp. garlic powder
5 tsp. paprika
3 tsp. onion powder

1. Mix together.

2. Store in a tightly covered jar or bottle.

Makes:

7 tsp.= 1.25 oz.
bought pkg.

Note:

This has no salt like
bought packages
do, so allow for
that when using it
to season a dish.

Homemade Vanilla Yogurt

2 quarts whole milk
1 Tbsp. unflavored gelatin
⅓ cup cold water

3 Tbsp. active yogurt
½ cup sugar *or* maple syrup
2 tsp. vanilla extract

Note:

1. Put milk in a 3- or 4-quart kettle. Heat to 180°.

2. When milk reaches 180°, set kettle in cold water and cool yogurt to 130°, stirring occasionally with wire whip.

3. While yogurt is cooling, put gelatin in cold water to soften.

4. Measure active yogurt, and sugar or maple syrup.

5. When milk has reached 130°, remove kettle from cold water. Stir in softened gelatin, active yogurt, and sugar or maple syrup. Stir well until everything is dissolved.

6. Put into glass bowls (I use two) and cover with plates. Keep warm for 8 hours. (I use my oven which has a pilot light, providing just the right temperature.)

7. The next morning add 1 tsp. vanilla to each bowl, gently mixing it in with an egg beater.

8. Cover and refrigerate yogurt. Gently whip it with a wire whip before serving to make it creamy.

9. Serve with fruit, use in smoothies, with cereal, and in parfaits. The options are many.

Note:

If you prefer Greek yogurt, do not add gelatin. Continue cooling yogurt for an hour or two after it reaches 130°. Then drain it through cheesecloth or another fine cloth for an hour, or until it's as thick as you want.

We like to make parfaits with this in individual glass dishes. First a layer of granola, followed by a layer of yogurt, then fruit of your choice, plus a sprinkle of granola on top.
Fresh fruit is good, but we also use canned pie filling in the winter-time.
We often eat this as dessert, or as a side dish for supper, our lighter meal.

Cream Cheese

2 quarts cream
1 packet direct-set mesophilic starter *or* 4 oz. prepared mesophilic starter
3 drops liquid rennet, diluted in ⅓ cup water
1 to 2 quarts water
salt, to taste, *optional*
herbs, to taste, *optional*

1. Heat cream to 86°, add starter, and mix thoroughly.

2. Add 1 tsp. diluted rennet and stir gently with an up and down motion.

3. Cover and let cream stand 12 hours at room temperature. A solid curd will form.

4. Heat water to 170°.

5. Add enough of hot water to the curd to raise its temperature to 125°.

6. Pour curd into colander lined with butter muslin or thin cloth.

7. Tie corners of cloth in a knot. Hang bag to drain until it stops dripping.

8. Put cheese in bowl. Add salt and herbs to taste, if desired.

9. Place cheese in molds and store in refrigerator.

10. Once cheeses are firm, unmold and wrap individually in cheese wrap. Store in refrigerator for 1 to 2 weeks.

A Good Family-Gathering Idea!

When siblings—or even good friends—gather together, ask each one to bring several bowls or jars of soups, enough to feed their families who will be joining the meal. When everyone is there, pour all the soups together into a large soup pot. Heat and enjoy! Serve with crackers and cheese.

Play Dough

1 cup all-purpose flour
2 tsp. cream of tartar
½ cup salt
1 cup water
1 Tbsp. vegetable oil
food coloring, *optional*

The salt in the dough will keep children from tasting or eating it.

1. Mix dry ingredients in saucepan.

2. Stir in water and oil.

3. Cook over low heat for about 5 minutes, stirring frequently until well blended.

4. Add coloring if desired.

5. When mixture forms a ball, roll it out on a board or countertop. Knead while as hot as possible until smooth.

6. Cool, then store in tight containers. It keeps well.

Bird Feed

1 cup lard *or* tallow
1 cup crunchy peanut butter
2½ cups dry rolled oats
3 cups cornmeal

¼ cup cracked sunflower
  seeds, *optional*
¼ cup raisins, *optional*

1. Melt lard or tallow.

Birds love it!

2. Stir in remaining ingredients.
It will be stiff, so you may need to mix it with your hands.

Relaxing, Herbal, Sleepy-Time Bath

2 Tbsp. dried chamomile
2 Tbsp. dried lavender
1 Tbsp. dried comfrey leaves
3 cups water

1. In saucepan, combine herbs and water. Simmer on low for about 5 minutes.

2. Remove from heat, cover, and let stand for 5 minutes.

3. Strain out herbs.

4. Pour liquid into bath water.

5. Mixture eases tension, relaxes muscles, and benefits the skin.

Grandma's Winter Tonic

3 cups elderberries
1 cup honey

1. Cover elderberries with water in saucepan. Bring to boil. Cover and simmer 30 minutes.

2. Using potato masher or back of spoon, press on berries to release all juices.

3. Strain juice into a glass jar or bowl.

4. Cool until lukewarm. Add honey, stirring until dissolved.

5. Pour syrup into quart jar or bottle. Keep in refrigerator.

Tip:

Take one dose per day during flu season to build up your immunity.

Daily dose:

1 tsp. for children; 1 Tbsp. for adults.

If you get a bad cold or flu, take the doses every 3 hours.

Natural Cleanser and Deodorant

2 Tbsp. dried lovage leaves and roots
¼ cup dried sage leaves
1 cup hot water
several drops lavender essential oil

1. Stir lovage leaves and roots and sage leaves into water.

2. Let stand 5 minutes.

3. Strain. Add several drops of oil to liquid. Splash underarms after a bath.

Index

Subscribe to Elsie's magazine—

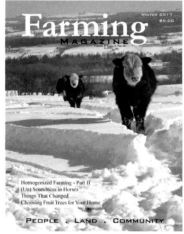

Many of the recipes in this terrific cookbook first appeared (in earlier versions) in *Farming Magazine*, of which Elsie Kline is the Gardening & Food Editor. You can be a subscriber, too!

Founded in 2001 by David and Elsie Kline, *Farming Magazine* is the only magazine helping small-scale farmers make a good living—and a good life—from the land. Why not join the conversation!

Farming Magazine celebrates the joys of farming well and living well on a small and ecologically conscious scale. It explores the intricate bonds connecting people, land, and community and

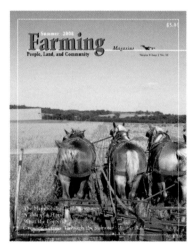

offers a hopeful vision for the future of farming in America. The magazine is created in the spirit of stewardship for the earth and regard for its inhabitants.

1 year (4 issues)—$18.00   2 years (8 issues)—$32.00

(Or send $5.00 for a sample copy)

Mail checks payable to Farming Magazine to P.O. Box 85, Mt. Hope, OH 44660.

For more information about this

book and other titles published by

Walnut Street Books, please visit

www.walnutstreetbooks.com.

About the Author

Elsie Kline lives with her husband David on an organic dairy farm in Ohio. She has always enjoyed all aspects of farm life—cooking, gardening, milking cows, and helping in the fields if necessary, as well as the joys of the natural world—birdwatching, wildflower walks, wading in the creek with her grandchildren, or a good softball game in earlier years.

She prefers preparing meals from her gardens and the farm, using only natural ingredients.

Elsie and David have three daughters—Kristine, Ann, and Emily; two sons—Timothy and Michael, 23 grandchildren, and 1 great-grandchild. Elsie and David are Old Order Amish.

Elsie writes "The Farm Home" columns in *Farming Magazine* and also co-edits the quarterly magazine, which she and David began publishing in 2001.